(great)

EMPLOYEES ONLY

great

EMPLOYEES ONLY

How Gifted
Bosses Hire
and De-Hire
Their Way
to Success

Dale Dauten

WILEY

John Wiley & Sons, Inc.

Published by John Wiley & Sons, Inc., Hoboken, New Jersey.

Published simultaneously in Canada.

For general information on our other products and services or for technical support, please contact our Customer Care Department within the United States at (800) 762-2974, outside the United States at (317) 572-3993 or fax (317) 572-4002.

Wiley also publishes its books in a variety of electronic formats. Some content that appears in print may not be available in electronic books. For more information about Wiley products, visit our web site at www.wiley.com.

A few segments of this book originally appeared, in somewhat different form, in the privately printed book, *The Laughing Warriors.*

Library of Congress Cataloging-in-Publication Data:

Dauten, Dale A.
    (Great) employees only : how gifted bosses hire and de-hire their way to
success / Dale Dauten.
        p.   cm.
    Includes index.
    ISBN-13: 978-0-470-00788-4 (cloth)
    ISBN-10: 0-470-00788-5 (cloth)
    1. Executive ability.   2. Employee selection.   3. Employees—Attitudes.
4. Management.   I. Title.
    HD38.2.D383   2006
    658.3′1—dc22
                                                            2006005315

Printed in the United States of America.

10 9 8 7 6 5 4 3 2 1

For Sandy,
again,
and still.

"It is, indeed, an observable fact that all leaders . . . all those who can get the best out of others, have always identified with high ideals, and this has added strength and scope to their influence. Though reason may sometimes condemn them, feeling clothes them in an aura of glory."
— Charles de Gaulle

●

"Lots of folks confuse destiny with bad management."
— Kin Hubbard

●

"Lighting one candle
with another candle —
Spring evening."
— Yosa Buson

●

"The world is a stage, but the play is badly cast."
— Oscar Wilde

Contents

ix

PART II
From *Employees* to *Allies*

PART III
The Graceful Art of De-Hiring

PART IV
Inspiring, Effortless Leadership
(The First Step in Hiring Great Employees)

PART V
Hiring Is What You Do So You Don't Have to Manage (and It's What You Do with Some of the Time You Save by Not Having to Manage)

PART VI
Understanding Bureaucrats, Upper Management, and Other Distractions

Preface

After studying hundreds of executives, here's my formula for effortless leadership success:

- 90 percent hiring (and de-hiring),
- 10 percent inspiring, and
- 0 percent management. (If an employee can't be inspired and needs managing, return to top.)

Notice that 90-10-0 is a formula for leadership success, not for a leader's time. It isn't that the most successful leaders devote no time to managing and spend nearly all their hours hiring and de-hiring; rather, their *success* is derived from their hiring, de-hiring, and inspiring, while the hours spent managing are essentially unnecessary and, thus, wasted.

Before we go any further, let's back up and consider the word in that formula that may be unfamiliar to you: *de-hiring*. It's a term I coined to describe a skill that great bosses possess but rarely discuss. A decade ago, as part of my search for the best bosses in America, I discovered a surprising fact about some of the country's great managers: They often have considerable turnover. This perplexed me. After all, if you're a great boss, you hire terrific people and create a great work environment that no one wants to leave, right? But employees were leaving— some of the best ones were being lured away to marvelous new jobs while those with less talent were leaving because the gifted boss was escorting them out, usually with such grace that they gladly moved on to a position better suited to their gifts.

This latter process fascinated me. These were not *brutally demanding bosses* who fired anyone who made a mistake; no, these were *lovably demanding bosses* who devoted themselves to helping every employee travel along his or her path. Those employees who left did so willingly, grateful for having been there. In other words, everyone was better off—those who stayed and those who left—and especially the boss who was able, in effect, to trade in second-rate employees for new stars, and in doing so, rapidly evolve a stronger team.

Let's consider the effects of putting this book out on your desk. If you are the sort of manager that this writer hopes to have as a reader—someone who's thoughtful and caring—then I suspect that one of your first thoughts on seeing the subtitle of this book was, "If the people on my team see the word 'de-hiring' they might worry that I'm going to get rid of them—what will it do to morale?"

(continued)

(Continued)

Good managers often hide books about firing people in the briefcase, as if they are management porn. That's not necessary here. Great-employees-only leadership is no-secrets leadership. In fact, if you have people on your team who are decent employees but who fall short of the level of excellence you are seeking for your team, then you want them to see this book on your desk. Here's what might happen:

> One insurance executive brought her assistant to one of my seminars where I included a section on de-hiring. A few weeks later the assistant came to the executive's office and said, "You're trying to de-hire me, aren't you?"
>
> The executive said, "No, I'm trying to help you become a star employee."
>
> The assistant eventually admitted that she didn't want to work that hard. That afternoon she went to human resources and arranged for a transfer. The executive was then free to hire a new assistant—one who yearned for a chance to join a high-wattage team.

If you find that your goals are greater than your staff, and you need to evolve to a higher-level of performance, then this book will help you be of help to everyone on your team. You will get better at assisting people in advancing along their personal paths, while simultaneously learning how to attract people traveling higher talent paths; after all, the best want to work with the best.

●

In an ideal world, you're an expansion team and you go out and win the World Series. Not gonna happen. As a boss you want to be loyal to the .220 hitter because he has a nice smile and tries hard, but you have to understand that HE WON'T TAKE YOU TO THE WORLD SERIES.

> —*Todd McFarlane, creator of Spawn comics, owner of McFarlane toys and part owner of the Edmonton Oilers*

●

De-hiring is not, however, enough. The parallel issue is this: Do the bosses who de-hire have a different approach to hiring? Absolutely. They readily de-hire because they have a talent pool from which to select fresh talent. They are masters of spotting and courting stars. Further, they attract the best because they don't just offer jobs, but admission to "circles of helping," where colleagues inspire one another to grow and blossom.

Ultimately, the skillful use of talent courtship along with de-hiring allows the gifted boss to create a team that everyone wants to be a part of, establishing a culture that does much of the hiring and de-hiring. What does that culture look like?

When a group of allies is working toward a worthy goal, it is often difficult for an outsider to guess who is the leader. Such a team doesn't seem to have a boss, and yet it needs one. I don't believe in "Hire good people and get out of the way." When it's a great-employees-only environment, the boss is *not* there to answer questions, but to ask them. The boss is not there to require compliance, but to inspire experimentation. The boss becomes a star by being a great audience to the team of all-stars. *The gifted boss doesn't get out of the way, but is the keeper of The Way, the one who sees what could be.*

●

To gain admission to a great-employees-only workplace requires an understanding of how gifted bosses think and work differently from typical bosses. To get there, we start by engaging the logic and philosophy of great employees only, then move more deeply into the essentials of implementation by considering 48 Wisdoms of Gifted Bosses.

Part 1

great

EMPLOYEES ONLY

90-10-0:
The Formula for
Leadership Success

Number 1

Hiring *Is* Motivation,
or
It's Less Work to Get 100 Percent Improvement than 10 Percent Improvement

The Tale of Two Bosses

Let's say we have two managers who, on the same day, take over identical teams. Both are bright and eager to excel. One has read all the management books on motivation; the other has just this book. In six months, the first manager will have increased productivity by 10 percent, maybe 20 percent. The second boss, using the great-employees-only (GEO) system, will have increased productivity by over 100 percent, while putting in one-third fewer hours at the office. Along the way, our second manager will have encountered less resistance, made more friends, learned more, and had much more fun.

Let's put some numbers to the experience of our imaginary pair. Say that each manager has four direct reports, and that we can perfectly measure how productive each manager is. (Economists use the word *utils* to represent units of utility, or usefulness. We'll just call them *units*.) So let's say each manager starts with a team that looks like this:

Assistant Manager A:	40 units
Assistant Manager B:	30 units
Assistant Manager C:	20 units
Assistant Manager D:	10 units
	100 units of output

Our first manager, as soon as he joins his new team, will work with each employee individually, bring in motivational tools, have pizza parties, and hand out T-shirts and balloons. A couple of the employees might think he's just another management glad-hander, but the other two work harder and soon, their output goes up by 20 percent. However, not everyone is improving, so the net increase, for the full team, might be 10 percent. Not bad. Exhausting work for the manager, and the employees who improve might backslide, but not bad.

Across town, our GEO boss faces an identical challenge. Instead of trying to spur on the employees, however, she determines that the weakest performer will not achieve the new expectations, and de-hires her. (That employee eagerly transfers to another department, better suited to her strengths, and her performance rises substantially. She will soon be telling people, "Changing departments was the best thing that ever happened to me.")

Dipping into her talent pool, our GEO boss brings in a new assistant manager who is far better than anyone currently on the team. So, the day the new person starts, the weakest performer, Assistant Manager D, is gone and the team looks like this:

Assistant Manager A:	40 units
Assistant Manager B:	30 units
Assistant Manager C:	20 units
Assistant Manager D:	(De-hired)
Assistant Manager E (New):	60 units
	150 units

But we're not done. Watching the old employee leave and the new star arrive has an impact on the other employees—a form of motivation that goes beyond mere lecturing or coaching. The old star learns from the new one, and soon equals him. The less proficient employees now see what their new manager expects. One ups her level, learning from the two stars, while the weakest employee decides he doesn't want to work that hard, and leaves, thus opening up another slot. Now we have this:

(First new hire) Assistant Manager E:	60 units
(Old star, improved) Assistant Manager A:	60 units
(Second new hire) Assistant Manager F:	50 units
(Old employee, improved) Assistant Manager B:	40 units
	210 units

Thus, we can see that output has more than doubled, presided over by a boss who devotes almost no time to managing, instead devoting her time to promoting the department in the company, getting her department the choice assignments, experimenting and learning, and spotting talent to add to her collection of allies. Meanwhile, her employees are not just better, but happier.

In other words, starting with an identical situation, she has a much better job—an easier time, yielding more success. And the employees who left her department—they are also among her allies, respecting her and feeling grateful to her for helping them find what they were meant to do.

•

Sounds simple? It is. . . . Or would be, if it were not for the forces of bureaucracy and mediocrity standing in line to fight you. However, if you are wise and if you are crafty and determined, you can learn to defeat them, and have a good laugh while doing so.

Number 2

You Can *Change* People, or You Can Change *People*

Getting improvements in attitude and output by managing people is achingly hard work. That's because you're trying to get people to change, and you have to cross a minefield of ancient-brain resistance and resentments.

Here is a description of two major (successful) management initiatives, as described by Charles Tombazian, Bill Heitzman, Stephen Brown, and Geoff Zwemke in *Pursuit of the Summit: Attracting and Retaining the Best Employees* (from the "Compete Through Service" symposium put on by Steve Brown of Arizona State University in 1999. *PowerNotes*, a service that summarizes business conferences, recorded the text.) Notice how dauntingly, numbingly difficult these build-better-employees approaches sound:

Both Larry Crosby, CEO of Symmetrics Marketing Corp., and Tony Rucci, former senior vice president of administration for Sears, quantify the effects of employee behavior and attitude on business results. They cite case study statistics substantiating the link between employee attitude, customer loyalty and profits. Crosby's study shows a 10 percent increase in employee commitment (usually reflected in positive behaviors) resulted in a 7 percent increase in customer loyalty, which in turn increased profitability by 5 percent. Rucci's case study is on his former company, Sears. There, a 5 percent improvement in employee attitudes about their jobs and the company resulted in a 1.3 percent improvement in customer retention, generating a 0.5 percent increase in revenue growth. Sound like small potatoes? With Sears' revenue in the billions, even a 0.5 percent increase equates to a tidy sum.

"Small potatoes?" the authors ask. Maybe not, in a giant operation. Their point was that improving employees improves business. My point in including that paragraph is to demonstrate how exhausting management can be. Imagine the effort it takes in a bureaucracy to get that 5 percent improvement in attitudes about jobs. Then, the improvement in customer retention is only a fraction of that increase . . . and so on. To me, that's opening up a small-potatoes farm. What we are looking for are revolutionary improvements, and that's going to take more than small management.

Number 3

The First Step to Finding Star Employees Is Believing That They Exist,
or
How to Make the Playing Field as Un-Level as Possible

You can spend a lot of time telling employees how you want them to behave, or you can do their jobs for them and demonstrate how you want it done, or you can hire a new role model and show them how a star employee looks and acts.

Some managers mistrust such star employees, fearing being overshadowed; other managers don't believe star employees exist. Both these beliefs are the result of spending too much time inside bureaucracies, where fear and mediocrity work together to create a "level playing field." Great-employees-only leaders detest "level"; their careers are devoted to running downhill. They want more talent on their side than anyone else. That's why they don't seek out mere "employees"; they want lifelong allies. More on that later in the book. For now, let's take a look at what one great new colleague can accomplish for an organization.

Cold Stone Creamery is a franchise company with over a thousand locations and growing rapidly, led by CEO Doug Ducey, a boyish charmer with a quick smile who has the wisdom and humility to surround himself with terrific talent. Listen as he tells us of the time when the company's cost of goods was rising and he seemed powerless to control it.

We buy a lot of stuff. If you want to be 'the ultimate ice cream experience,' you can't use just any cookie in your Cookies & Cream; you use Oreos. And that's repeated across a lot of items. As we grew, our costs were rising. Our franchisees were feeling it, and when our franchisees feel it, I feel it right here [grabs cell phone on his belt]. This starts vibrating.

So we went in search of the best supply chain vice president in the country. We looked at people from all the bigger chains, and we finally found Bruce Burnham, who'd been with Burger King.

We were late to the hire. I'd been focused on management, marketing, and financing and I hadn't kept up with distribution and purchasing. We had a person in charge who was good and working hard—she was purchasing—but we had grown beyond her experience. We had become a different company from when she started.

How good was Bruce? Well, *within a year of his joining Cold Stone, a franchisee had "We ♥ Bruce" buttons printed up and passed them out at a national meeting, where they were merrily worn by grateful Cold Stone owners.*

I spoke with Bruce to inquire how he had come to be so beloved, and he explained that he'd gotten the company to add ice cream-mix plants and reduce the number of distribution centers, all part of a strategy to build the supply chain infrastructure. When I asked what difference that had made, he leaned back and said, casually, "About a dollar a case in distribution."

"How many cases?" I wondered.

"About three million this year." Then he added, "Plus there's the freight costs, which are down about two dollars a case."

"How many of those?"

"About a million and a half."

He continued on with food costs, but I think you see the point—we're already up to $6 million. Because those savings are passed along to franchisees, you can understand the "I ♥ Bruce" buttons—I'd be wearing one, wouldn't you? If you don't have employees you want to put on silly buttons with hearts, then you're not hiring right.

Number 4

You Can Lead an
Employee to Water,
but If You Find One
Who Knows a Better
Path to the Water,
Shut Up and Get
a Bucket

Let's examine the role of ego in leadership by considering the case of the football coach, Buddy Ryan. He was part of three teams that reached the Super Bowl, and as a head coach in Philadelphia, he had a winning record. So, when he was hired as head coach of the Arizona Cardinals and vainly declared on arriving, "You have a winner in town," he was correct on one level. However, he was soon proven very wrong: His record with the Cardinals was 12–20. More important, he was wrong on a philosophical level: He thought that his management would determine the team's success. By believing that *he* could *make* the team win, he was, in fact, set up to be a loser.

●

The reason that the formula for leadership success is 90-10-0 is that, no matter who the leader is, the employees still have to make a decision as to how much effort to give. That effort is a percentage of their energy, talent, and knowledge. Employees can indeed give more than 100 percent—surrounded by the right coworkers, they are lifted to a higher plane of accomplishment. Talent inspires talent; that's one reason the best want to work with the best—to be challenged, lifted, and educated.

Success is a gift that the best employees bestow on the organization. Being worthy of that gift is the goal of the wise leader.

Part II

great
EMPLOYEES ONLY

From *Employees* to *Allies*

Number 5

Those Aren't Employees (or Friends, Enemies, Family, or Students)— Those Are Allies

What is the ideal relationship between manager and employees? Let's examine several models, starting with the least effective one and working our way up.

The dreariest of management mind-sets is employees as *the enemy*, thus making the boss a kind of occupation-force general. Assume the worst, and you're sure to get it. This seems obvious, but I'm certain you've encountered such managers. Most would never admit that they think of employees as enemies; rather, they believe that employees "need watching" and find humor in statements like "this business would be okay except for the people." They build systems solely for preventing mistakes, which erodes positivism, and they end up thinking like prison wardens instead of leaders.

Next up the ladder is the management mentality where employees are *hired hands*. The boss is the rancher and the employees are the help. (Thinking of yourself as a *coach* and employees as the *players* is a related mind-set.) Employees come and go and some are better than others, but they are there to have specific responsibilities and be under the close direction of the boss. These tend to be managers who feel superior to their employees, believing that they are smarter and that they could perform each task better than the person doing it, if only they could clone themselves. (Then again, if you try to control everything, you can't hire—or at least can't keep hired—the best employees, the ones who don't need managing.)

Dan Schweiker, the co-CEO of China Mist Tea, tells us, "When I talk with fellow executives, many of them spend time complaining about their employees and how much time managing them takes. I ask them why they try to control everything and they say, 'I can do my employees' jobs better than they can.' And I think, 'Boy, did you hire the wrong people.'"

The next rung on our ladder is the metaphor of *family*. The problem here is that the boss sees himself as dad or herself as mom and the result isn't a family, it's a parental model of management, based on control. Worse yet, the family notion invites all the Freudian maelstroms into the workplace. In my experience, the bosses who say their employees are "like family" usually end up with employees who are like insolent teenagers—resentful and eager to move on.

> I met one "mom" manager with a staff of three younger women who told me with emotion, "I call them 'my girls' because they are like daughters to me. I'd do anything for them and they'd do anything for me. I can't get them to take time off they're so loyal to me." Later, when I met with the staff and mentioned that last remark, they laughed. One explained, "We always try to all be here for each other because none of us can stand being here alone with her."

Next are bosses who think of employees as *friends*. There are some gifted bosses in this group, and they are so adroit that it works for them. Still, there are the obvious problems—a tendency to take advantage of the relationship, and a possible blindness to mediocrity that comes from being too comfortable. There is, I believe, another concern, one I've never seen commented on: If you have employee/friends, then you tend to hire people you like. Hiring people like you is an awful habit—we all need people with opposite skills to counterbalance us, and how likely is it that opposite skills are housed in a similar personality? Without being conscious of it, most bosses, even good ones, hire for similarity instead of hiring for difference. But I want to go well beyond overcoming that habit and consider something far more difficult for most people to apprehend: Make a goal of hiring some people you don't like (or at least, people with whom you could never be friends).

You need people with interests that diverge from your own. You need passionate people of every ilk—geeks and introverts, clowns and intellectuals, detail people and idea people, cat people and dog people, atheists and evangelists. So, if you like everyone on your staff well enough that you would be friends with them outside of work, either you have an astounding capacity for friendship or else your hiring is too narrow.

Instead of hiring people you like, the criterion of most gifted bosses is *hiring people you can admire.* Not admire for their lifestyle or personality, but admire for their work and their commitment to it. This brings us to the top of the metaphor ladder—employees as *allies.*

Having allies changes the nature of the employment relationship. For one thing, you don't have to try to select or modify personalities—you free yourself to assemble a diverse team of talents who don't even have to like one another, all just have to be committed to helping . . . not helping you, but helping the team . . . committed to a circle of helping. You eventually reach the point when one ally can say of another, "She'd drive me crazy if I had to live with her, but, hey, the customers *love* her." Or "He's a loner and doesn't join in the company events, but he produces the most amazing results."

When employees become allies, it also moves the relationship beyond the current hierarchy. When I did the research for *The Gifted Boss*, I was surprised to find how fluid employment became when you are dealing with high-level talent—a star employee left and eventually hired the old boss, or an employee left and came back, and so on. There is a commitment not just to an employment relationship, but to one another, to a lifelong alliance of talent.

Number 6

Those Aren't *Former Employees*—Those Are *Graduates*

Thinking in terms of lifelong allies makes some startling alterations in the mind-set of a manager. Of all the wisdoms of gifted bosses, the one that seems to have the most immediate impact is also the shortest; it's just one word, really—*graduates*. That's how Dan Schweiker (the co-CEO of China Mist Tea that we met earlier) refers to people who have worked for him and then moved on, whether they were stars hired away to a better job or employees who were de-hired into better situations. When I most recently sat down with Dan, I told him of the response to his concept of "graduates." He seemed surprised that others hadn't already thought of it, then lit up as a memory came to him: "One of the graduates—one of our Regional managers who left 10 years ago—I just heard from last Friday. He called with a lead for us."

When asked how it was that that particular employee had left the company, Dan said, "He got a better offer. We'd trained him well and he needed to go with a bigger company. He needed to learn things we didn't know how to teach him." Now *that's* how a gifted boss thinks. No animosity about an employee's leave-taking, like the parental boss would have; no negative spin that a hired-hand boss or a bitter employees-as-enemies boss would have; no feeling of abandonment like the friend boss. Instead, because that employee was treated as an ally, he was a graduate. A professor wouldn't resent the student for graduating; rather, the professor would delight in the student's accomplishments. And what better example of the benefits of having, instead of a resented ex-employee, a lifelong ally: *Ten years later and the graduate is still calling up with a lead for a new customer.*

Dan has a similar relationship with de-hired employees, or as he puts it, the ones he "helped into their futures." He easily separates the performance from the person, saying, "Almost everyone has a place they fit into. My first two or three jobs I didn't fit. Only when I got into this business did I feel at home."

The upshot is that Dan is in touch with most nearly all his graduates, regardless of how or why they left the company.

●

Another advantage of having lifelong allies is that it enables a no-secrets approach to working together. You don't have to define being a "team player" as pretending that you are delighted with everything about the job and intend to spend your whole career together. Late in 2005, Bethany Murray, my editor at King Features (which syndicates my newspaper columns) announced that she was leaving. I was sorry to hear it—we'd had a great relationship and her talents had spared me many mistakes as well as sharpened many of my comments. Bethany was, I learned, taking a job at Cornell, near where she grew up. So, great for her, but I was sorry for her manager, Chris Richcreek, and asked her how he was taking the news. She said, "Chris helped me get the job. He's known for two years that I wanted to move back to upstate New York." When I said something complimentary about Chris's open-mindedness, she responded:

His goal is to see the people he knows happy. I'd get discouraged, thinking I'd never find a job near my home and he'd say, "You're great and when the time is right, it will happen." I'd even copy him on job ads and ask his opinion. When the Cornell job came up, he wrote to them for me. I knew I had the job when he called them. He thinks I can do anything and I knew if he'd talked to them, they'd offer me the job.

They did, and Bethany concluded our conversation by asking me to turn in my columns early—she was working ahead before she left to make the transition easier for her boss, Chris, and whomever he chose to replace her.

Now you might wonder if Chris was doing some skillful de-hiring, but that wasn't the case. I spoke to him and he was genuinely sorry to see Bethany leave her job. He had the GEO-boss attitude, saying, "There's your life and there's your job. I try to help do all I can to make employees lives easier. Bethany was happy here, but I wanted her to find where she would be happi*est*."

As allies, the two were able to establish a bond that outlasts employment at King Features. I wouldn't be surprised if those two work together again, and I'm certain they will help each other. If Bethany had to sneak around looking for work, she might have simply quit and Chris would have lost a star employee sooner. If he'd been resentful of her leaving, he would have lost not just an employee, but an ally, a talented person who might be a future employee at some new company, and certainly a useful contact, a source of talent or ideas out of Cornell, perhaps even a possible source of job leads for him in the future. She didn't quit; she graduated.

Number 7

You Never Get
Rid of Anyone

Robert Thurman once offered me a Zen notion that might be helpful to our thinking here. (He teaches at Columbia, was the first Westerner to become a Tibetan Buddhist monk, has written some marvelous books, and, by the way, is the father of the actress, Uma Thurman.) Professor Thurman—I can't bring myself to call him Bob, even though he told me to when I talked with him—says that in Zen logic, if you have been reincarnated an infinite number of times, then everyone you meet has been, in some life or other, your mother. That bizarre premise has popped into my mind a hundred times since, especially when I encounter someone who tests my patience. If it were my mother, would I find a way to understand and replace frustration with compassion?

If you could evaluate each employee as if she (even if she's a he) were once your mother, you'll have to help her travel along her life's path, whether or not it diverges from your own. It might also help you recall that the people in your life, even the most frustrating ones, are there for a reason. You are their teacher, just as they are yours. And they'll be back, one way or another; or they'll remain with you as a lesson learned. You never get rid of anyone.

Number 8

It's Not Closure That's Needed—It's Aperture

One of the most popular words of recent decades is "closure." Well, if you never really get rid of anyone, there is no closure. If everything happens for a reason, everything is a lesson and lessons need no closure. Instead of seeking closure, the best bosses— the best *people*—are the ones striving to remain open to life. Said another way, the goal is not closure, but aperture.

As an anonymous Japanese poet put it:

> My barn having burned
> To the ground
> I can now see
> The moon.

Number 9

How Two Allies (a Great Employee and a Gifted Boss) Find Each Other

If we are to find lifelong allies among our employees, we need to know all we can about how they think and work, and especially what they look for in an employer. Let's consider how a great employee goes about finding a job. Let's listen to Ellen Barredo, who relocated to a new city and conducted *not* a mere job search, but a great organization/ gifted boss search. Here, in her own words, is Ellen's experience:

Nine years ago I moved home to St. Louis. I had been living in Minneapolis. I am in the retail nursery industry. I had worked for the prestigious Bachman's Nursery in Minneapolis, a family business for more than a hundred years with a wonderful historical story. (Stories sell things!)

Back in St. Louis, I was not locating a business with the high standards of knowledge, customer services, sales, merchandising, exacting tidiness, a tropical green house and, most of all, an owner who would treat his employees with respect. I was secret-shopping the nurseries in town and then I found Timbercreek and Bob Specker. He had a family business he created, displayed a passion for the industry and seemed to fit all of my requirements. I decided to make it known to Bob that I would like to be considered for employment. I interviewed with Bob and met with him several times through the fall season. Fall in St. Louis is not the time to be searching for a job in the green industry unless you want to work on a landscape crew! Right before Thanksgiving I was almost stir crazy and contacted Bob again. He had me come in and I suppose he could see my intention was to get employed somewhere soon. Bob took a risk. He offered me a job with conditions. I was required to be industry certified as I had been with the state of Minnesota, and in order to keep my job I had to identify one area of the business that needed improvement and enact those improvements.

I took the job, the challenge, identified the greenhouse as a source of needed improvement, enacted change, and got certified. I accomplished Bob's goals and more, and kept my job.

Ellen Barredo went on to say that her gifted boss sold the business and retired young, allowing her to find another great boss. "My only regret," she adds, "is that I didn't get to work with him longer."

Wonderful story, no? Don't you love how Ellen's enthusiasm comes through even in her description of her work—"Stories sell things!" Let's be sure we didn't miss any of the lessons this great employee has to teach:

- Gifted bosses create places where people want to work, places with stories to tell.
- Gifted bosses are always hiring, even in the off-season.
- Great employees are almost never in the traditional job market—they're good and they know it, so they instead "make it known" that they are available. Notice how Ellen Barredo became a "secret shopper," not a job hunter. (Here we see another reason why it's "great employees *only*"—you can't afford to have a great prospect, whether customer or employee, put off by encountering even a single mediocrity.)
- Gifted bosses don't have mere employees; they have allies. They can say to an employee, "Find something you do better than we do and make us better."

When you find a gifted boss and great employee coming together, it is something much finer than a job being filled; it is a talent pool getting deeper and broader, a growing of the group brain.

Number 10

Assume the Best, Part I: The Art of Being a True Ally

When you see a gifted boss and a great employee working together, helping one another, that old expression "chemistry" is likely to come to mind. I prefer "chemistry" to the other common metaphor for employees joining a team — "fit." The better employees are not like jigsaw puzzles, with rigid edges needing to be figured out and fitted in, but are chemicals that change the composition of that to which they are added.

Let's look at what happens when a young star employee is recruited by a gifted boss. The employee is Renie Anderson, of the Arena Football League (AFL). The gifted boss is the AFL's commissioner, David Baker.

The commissioner hired Renie directly out of college to be his assistant. She says, "I did everything from answering phones to ordering office supplies. I had no set responsibilities; I was the keeper of all things." But, more than just carrying out assignments, she knew she was in a position to learn and grow: "I'd volunteer. I was a sponge. I'd take any assignment and run with it."

Renie was promoted to be manager of consumer products and after a few years, she was given the title she still holds, senior director of corporate sales. She has spent nearly a decade with the AFL and made this remarkable statement: "I see the passion in Commissioner Baker and choose to believe. I'm a believer. I choose to love what I do." She added, "I like to have a challenge every day. We get a new sponsor and my first thought is, 'What's next?'"

It's easy to become cynical in corporate life, to believe that you are being used and manipulated. It's easy *because it's true*—motivation is a form of manipulation and the art of management is simply the art of using people wisely and well. So, it makes sense that some employees would become eye-rolling doubters. But the great employees choose to believe that their employers want the best for their employees and customers. Why? Because *that's true, too*. It's true because great employees seek out employers they can believe in, and then resist the temptation to doubt those employers. They want to work with the best, find the best, and then *assume the best.*

In any organization, there are undercurrents of doubt, questions about management and how decisions are made. There are jealousies and intrigues. And how do great employees deal with them? They assume the best.

That's easy to do when there is no evidence to the contrary. It was the evil genius of Shakespeare's great villain, Iago, to come up with a bit of evidence—a handkerchief slipped to a supposed lover. And with that, Othello came to see what his mind was now looking for—evidence—which he soon found. However, it is the genius of great employees to tune their minds to the positive, to hear what they want to hear, and what they want to hear is the best interpretation of what goes on in the organization.

I have seen purposeful naivety used for overcoming negative evidence of every kind. I once wrote one of my newspaper columns on what I called "Kanter's Law" (for Rosabeth Kanter of the Harvard Business School): "Every project looks like a failure in the middle." I heard this story in response, from a young man named Rod Fielder of Moraine, Ohio:

I recently completed work on a million dollar movie that was made with the help of a saying of mine—

"I'm not smart enough to realize I can't succeed."
*I came up with it because of all the people that
rationalize they can't do something because they
don't have the tools, capabilities, connection or whatever else that holds them back.*

•

Later, when researching this book, I heard a
salesperson who we'll meet later, Dessa Eschmann,
describe one of her sales efforts:

*I was calling the owner of a store who told me to
call him after 8:00 on a Friday evening. I called at
8:15. He told me to call back in an hour. I called
at 9:15. He told me to call in an hour. I called him at
10:30 and he finally talked with me. If someone
tells me to call at a certain time, I do.* I never think
they're trying to get rid of me. I believe whatever
they tell me.

In observing other high-producer salespeople, I
see that same attitude, and it amounts to "assume
the best." And it's just as true of gifted bosses.
So, when you see a gifted boss and a great employee
together, you are seeing the chemistry of trust,
manifested in a mutual assuming of the best. They
look for evidence of trustworthiness, and they
find it.

Before we leave this section, I have to pass along a little story about what can happen when an employee assumes the worst. John Ball, an old friend and colleague, is a partner in a nifty architectural firm, Oz Architects in Scottsdale. He's the sort of boss who appreciates his employees and often makes efforts to demonstrate that appreciation. One of the little things he did, shortly before Thanksgiving one year, was to set up a table by the entrance to the firm's offices, and to greet employees as they entered in the morning, offering them juice and donuts and thanking them for working for Oz Architects. It was one of those little gestures that make him beloved by all those who work with him . . . well . . . *almost* everyone.

Standing by the door that morning, chatting with the staff well after most employees had arrived, a straggler came in, an employee who'd just started a couple of months earlier and barely knew John. When John greeted him, juice and donuts extended, the young employee pushed past him, visibly upset. It turns out that he was assuming the worst, believing John was mocking him for being late like one of those bosses who says, "I'm so glad you could join us this morning, Mary." The employee was so offended by John's greeting and presumed insult that he found a cardboard box, filled it with his possessions, and huffed out.

This turned out for the best, of course. An employee who thinks the worst of management would not fit at Oz Architects. So, I guess we could say that here was the first recorded case of de-hiring via donuts.

Number 11

Assume That the Best Employees ALWAYS KNOW

As reported in *The Economist*, Christian Keysers of the University of Groningen (Netherlands) completed an experiment in which he:

put his volunteers in a brain scanner and wafted disgusting odours such as rancid butter and rotten eggs into their nostrils. The odours activated part of the brain called the anterior insula. He then played film clips of people's faces registering disgust to his volunteers, and found activity in exactly the same part of the brain.

The conclusion was that we have "mirror neurons" that involve "the same neural circuitry that we require to have those experiences and emotions ourselves." So, watching someone be disgusted is disgusting. The same would be true for other emotions as well. What does that have to do with business? Well, it explains a lot about the success and failure of certain salespeople and certain leaders. We feel what they feel. Our brains connect, nonverbally. We see sour-faced leaders and they lead us to sourness. On the other hand, we all love to watch leaders "light up," and we feel—literally—their electricity.

As I've gotten to visit high-wattage workplaces around the country, one of the first things I notice is that they are full of laughter. I've visited many playful workplaces and have come to believe that this is the natural state of organizations, if management doesn't screw it up. In order not to screw it up, it helps to understand a bit about humor.

The psychologist Robert Provine has researched humor, and actually went around eavesdropping on conversations, recording what he called "naturally occurring human laughter." He and his graduate students ended up gathering information on 1200 instances, and here's Provine's conclusion:

Less than 30 percent of the laughter in our sample was a response to anything resembling a formal effort at humor. Even our "greatest hits," the funniest of the 1,200 prelaugh comments, were not necessarily howlers: "You don't have to drink, just buy us drinks" and "Do you date within your species?"

●

Provine concluded this: "Mutual playfulness, in-group feeling and positive emotional tone—not comedy—mark the social setting of most naturally occurring laughter."

So, how do you go about setting a positive emotional tone? One of the ways David Baker, the commissioner of the AFL, does so is by having a group of volunteers he calls the "fun police" plan group events, like going to the bowling alley, or organizing a parasailing expedition, or games of touch football.

Lesser bosses may hear such stories and imitate similar work breaks, only to find that their employees treat the events as just another chore. What makes the difference? It is management's underlying motivation—is it simply to manipulate employees or to celebrate them? Great employees always know. Always. In the commissioner's case, he insisted, "My people get more done with fewer resources than people at any company," then added this beautiful sentiment, "We need to let them know we love them."

I can believe that the employees feel loved. It isn't the trips to the bowling alley, but rather, the commissioner's concern about their being part of something and sharing in its success. The employees aren't just working for a growing organization, but for a leader committed to the growth of every employee. David says, "If your receptionist is growing, then so is your company."

He then spoke proudly of the people who had gone from entry-level jobs to executive positions. He was proud to be part of their success, and he understood that their success was his success.

That's how you get to be the fastest growing organization in your industry, with team values up 40-fold from when David took over. You don't get there by managing, but by hiring and inspiring, by showing the people around you that you love them and by believing that (this is worth repeating) *"If your receptionist is growing, then so is your company."* They always know.

Number 12

What's a Great Employee Worth?

In my search for the best bosses in the world, one of those closest to meeting all of the criteria is Kip Tindell, president of The Container Store chain. The pay of their store personnel is double the industry average. Sounds like a financial disaster, right? But Kip has bet the company on a belief that has become one of the company's foundation principles: "One great person equals three good people."

Following that logic, you can pay a great employee double and still come out ahead. And think what it does for customers, to encounter only great employees.

Kip says that the philosophy has become "self-propelling," which means, "hiring someone not conspicuously great would be a disappointment to all." Notice that phrase: "conspicuously great." When a writer from *Fortune* magazine did a story on The Container Store for their "Best Places to Work" issue, he was taken by the enthusiasm of the workers, but he never could figure out just why they were so happy. What he failed to understand is that The Container Store hires people who love to work and puts them with others of like mind.

Kip insists, "Great employees liberate us to bring in products that others can't sell." So, you put these self-propelled people together with innovative merchandise, and you create a better shopping experience, one where people come away with products they love—products they tell their neighbors about.

We concluded earlier that hiring is motivation, and that the best employees are self-managing, so hiring replaces managing, and now we see that hiring is marketing, as well. So, they are not just employees, but managers and marketers—triple the benefit to the company.

Part III

great

EMPLOYEES ONLY

The Graceful Art of De-Hiring

Number 13

Replacing People Is so Hard for Most Bosses That They Don't Do Enough of It

There are two tasks of a leader, one at either end of the zone of competence: management tasks and leadership tasks. Most management tasks are spent at the lower end, defining acceptable behavior, trying to correct problems, enforcing policies. However, the excitement comes at the upper end, inspiring new definitions of what is possible. As you move toward the higher end, some employees cling to the bottom level of performance, crying, "It's not fair, I'm doing acceptable work." They don't soar, they burrow. They're bureaucrats who like it at the bottom, and they do not intend to move up with you. What to do with them? Doing *something* (it would be easy to look the other way) is important—so important that I want you to think about the next two wisdoms before we move ahead to the graceful art of de-hiring.

Number 14

You Are Becoming Your Coworkers

We all know that we tend to take on traits from those around us; however, we like to think we make a choice in what we pick up, that we choose our role models. You might even go so far as to assume that because you are the boss, that employees will become like you. True. Nevertheless, at the same time, you are taking on their traits. Those around us pull on our personalities like the planets affecting each other's orbits. You may be the biggest planet in your solar system, but all the other orbits influence your orbit.

●

"If there are twelve clowns in a ring, you can jump in the middle and start reciting Shakespeare, but to the audience, you'll just be the thirteenth clown" (Adam Walinsky).

●

Every person in your department makes a statement about you as a manager, especially the best and worst. Every employee is the department. Every employee is you.

> David Allen, who is now with IBM Engineering and Technology Services, reminisced for us about making an instant job decision:
>
>> I once interviewed with an aerospace electronics firm located near the city where I grew up. I was quite excited with the prospect of moving back. My hopes were shattered completely when I was introduced to the technical lead of the department to which I would be assigned, if hired. It was my old lab partner from a college physics course. I knew from the moment I recognized him that I would never work for a company that considered him capable of being technical or leading anything. At the end of the day, I went back to my job far from my home town and declined the job offer.

You may never know how much a single employee is pulling down the department; no, you're preoccupied, getting your lines from Shakespeare just right.

Number 15

A Meeting Moves at the Pace of the Slowest Mind in the Room

When it comes to moving together as a team, the group IQ is not an average; it is the lowest person's IQ . . . or EQ or any other Q. You may well have a human speed bump in your midst—the one who literally cries out, "Slow down." That is the speed at which you all move—the slowest person's speed. Thus, everyone else in the room is bored and wasting time.

Combining this meeting-pace realization with the previous one, about becoming your coworkers, we can conclude that a mediocre employee in your group is more than one mediocre employee—he or she is a human multiplier-effect, to the downside. If you have even one mediocre employee you have announced to

(continued)

(Continued)

the world that mediocrity is okay by you, while conceding that you are willing to slow the entire group for the sake of the worst employee.

Thus, allowing that one person to stay is not being kind or generous; it's dangerous. It's dangerous for the individual, who knows, at some level, he or she is doing second-rate work, and you are locking that person into mediocrity, and it is dangerous for the group, which is slowed and distracted and begins to wonder about clowns.

Number 16

Firing Takes Guts—De-Hiring Requires Heart

There are executives who believe in firing and lay-offs. They congratulate themselves on having gotten hold of Darwin's logic. They have convinced themselves that by getting rid of people, they are guiding the organization's evolution. What they preside over is survival, not evolution. De-hiring is evolution; firings are destructive and usually turn into devolution.

In 2003, Boston University paid its newly hired president $1.8 million *not* to come to work. The university search team had offered the job to a former government official when it learned that, once in the president's office, he planned to replace all the current leadership. The university paid the $1.8 million as a contract buyout, and I think they got themselves a good deal. There is no "clean sweep" in firings and layoffs—it's always a mess.

David Bruno, an executive with the executive recruiting firm DHR International, tells the
tale of two new division presidents for one retail
chain. The first new one started, on his first day,
by firing all the other executives, dozens of
them, and did so in the most offensive way possible, with police escorts. That president lasted
a year, before being replaced by a woman
with what I think of as a leadership-by-asking-
questions style. Bruno describes the change in the
organization:

*The day the old president left you could feel
the change; it was like the entire company had been
holding its breath ever since the firings and the police escorts. The new president started and people
stopped worrying and started doing what's right.
They relaxed and when they did, they starting doing
their best work.*

•

There is a huge difference between surviving
and thriving. Darwinian management is based on
mere survival, recalling Tennyson's description of
nature as "red of tooth and claw." However, in organizational life, frightened people devote a large pro-
portion of their time to second-guessing, making
surviving anti-thriving.

As executive recruiter Julie Breninger told me:

> There are organizations that just can't make mistakes, which means that they just can't make decisions. I've had them interview candidates 10 times, asking the same questions over and over. They think they're being careful, but they just confuse themselves. I had one great candidate—who would have been a star for the company if they had gotten him—call me after the fourth time he went there for interviews and say, "I'm withdrawing my name. They can't make a decision and I'm not going to work at a place that can't make a decision."

There is no such thing as a painless layoff or firing. Managers about to "let people go" get nervous, and often combat the nervousness by getting angry or defensive; then, as they hear horror stories from the human resources (HR) or Legal department, any hope for civility leaks away. Even in the ideal case, the employee is going to be hurt and offended. (The sole, sad exception would be where management is so awful that people are relieved to be forced to do what they should have done years before.) Let's look at the ideal case of someone about to be laid off.

The woman we'll call "Annie" is a bright, personable, and talented employee. She is good at what she does and knows it. Here's a bit of my conversation with her about being laid off:

Annie: I got my review one day—I got the maximum ratings and maximum raise—and the next day I got laid off. The company was having financial trouble and had to lay off 75 people.

DD: But you knew it wasn't personal, because all the other people were being laid off, and you knew they loved your work.

Annie: *The hell it wasn't personal.* I got laid off and *I'm the one* who had to go home and tell my family.

DD: And what did your husband [the owner of a thriving business] say?

Annie: That it was for the best. That we didn't need the money and I could do what I'd been wanting to, go back and take some more college courses, and try some new things.

DD: So, no money issues, and you got to do what you'd been wanting to do. So, it worked out okay, right? It was all for . . .

Annie: *No! I was forced out of a job I loved. I felt damaged.*

I repeat that conversation as evidence that when it's a good job and a good person, it's never easy, not when it's layoffs or firings. It takes guts to tell people to leave, and that's why many managers look the other way and wait too long.

The prior example was, as I suggested, an "ideal" case—money was not an issue, and there was not an element of personal failure. Let's look at a more typical example of a firing/layoff, this from a woman who asked that I simply refer to her in print as "Linda":

I was fired from a job as executive director of a non-profit organization without any warning or without any explanation. The bad news came to me at a board of directors meeting the day before the Christmas party (which I had arranged) and just as we had begun to receive major contributions from a new fund-raising campaign that I had designed. It was particularly disheartening because I had left a great job and moved across the country for what I thought was this exciting new opportunity, and had pulled my daughter out of school in the middle of the year and up-rooted my 93-year-old mother.

Getting fired like this turned out to be somewhat of a financial disaster for me, and also created major challenges in terms of my career path. It had a tremendously negative impact on my daughter and mother. Though I was employed again within four months, I never have been able to get back on to the path I had mapped out for myself.

I do believe that the bad things that happen to us in life create opportunities to learn and grow and also add greatly to our ability to empathize with others. However, I think I would have been able to gain more from this personal disaster if the board members who fired me had provided me with some concrete information on why they were letting me go. Then I would have known more about the aspects of my job performance that needed improving. As it was, the whole thing was a mystery and I could only guess about what the problems might have been. Without the benefit of specific feedback on my failings in the job, I may still be carrying forward some traits as a manager, which makes me a less effective employee.

The people who fired Linda may have felt that they were improving the organization, maybe even evolving it. However, we see that Linda did not share in the evolution because she never knew why she was fired. It's even possible that the firing had nothing to do with her but was a matter of cronyism or some other organizational politics. On the other hand, she is left to wonder if she had a weakness to which she was blind, or if she still does. One of the glories of de-hiring is that there are no mysteries— the process is a laboratory for personal experimentation, insight, and growth.

We know that the majority of employees who are "let go" are going to end up saying, "It was the best thing that ever happened to me." So, while being fired may feel like being left behind on the ice floe, it's actually the first passage to looking back in satisfaction. Shouldn't a *leader* help lead people through that passage without pain, anger, and damage to their reputations or self-esteem?

●

With firing, struggling or difficult employees are told to leave. With de-hiring, those same employees are invited to stay, but only if the conditions are right for the person and the team. De-hiring, at its simplest, can look like this:

At a meeting with a group of insurance agents where I presented de-hiring strategies, one of the agents, Christy Chatham, recalled that she'd had a young woman working for her whose performance had declined into mediocrity. She said to that employee one day, "Are you happy?"

They had a brief conversation that left Cathy disappointed, feeling she hadn't gotten anywhere. However, the next morning the employee said, "Your question prompted me to rethink where I'm going with my life. I had a talk with my parents and they are going to help me go back to college full-time." Employer and employee hugged, both happy. The young student is still a client of that insurance agent and gladly reports on her progress.

Remember that we must *assume the best* and that *employees always know*. Done improperly, without the employee's best interests in mind, questions such as "Are you happy?" aren't part of the de-hiring process, they are just badgering an employee. If so, they are just a firing scam and can lead to anger, resentments, and lawsuits. Firing is telling employees that they are wrong for the organization; de-hiring is helping employees do (or find) what's right for themselves and the organization.

You often hear people talk about "having the guts to fire someone." Firing takes guts; de-hiring takes heart.

Number 17

Assume the Best, Part II: The Genius Lurking Inside

When I had the chance to meet with executives from the PetSmart chain, I asked if they had a store manager who was renowned inside the organization for his staff and hiring. They sent me to David Rains, store manager of one of the Las Vegas locations. David has an appealing openness about employees, embodying the "aperture" not "closure" mind-set, especially evident in his willingness to salvage employees. He says, "I take transfers. I take people who need a second chance." He explains, "They might have been at a store that was too busy or too slow, or just wasn't the right environment or situation for them. I'm open to working with anyone."

Here we see one of the striking differences between a Darwinian manager and the GEO leader.

The Darwinian has no time for "failures," but the GEO leader has an open mind and a large heart and is willing to look for the genius inside those who are struggling or unhappy elsewhere.

One such boss, Roy Vallee, CEO of Avnet, has given the "aperture" process a name in his company, calling it the "two-strike rule." If an employee isn't first-rate, the first assumption is that something is wrong with the chemistry, not the person. So, the employee is transferred to another manager. If that doesn't solve the problem then, as Roy puts it, "We know that some of those people would work out on a third try, but we're not an employment agency."

Another gifted boss, John Opland, when working for a furniture store chain in the Northwest, offered to take any management trainee that the other managers didn't want, as if his department had a corporate Statue of Liberty out front. His system was simple and is the essence of de-hiring.

He'd list goals for his new employee, along with a speech that we can boil down to this:

I know it wasn't going well for you before, but let's change that. Here's what it takes to be a star. I think you can achieve these goals, and do so in three months. Do you agree? You'll either be a star or move on and find the place that's right for you. What do you need from me to accomplish your goals?

This puts employees in charge of their futures, and there is no question when they are succeeding and when they aren't, especially when John holds regular meetings to assess their progress and offer his aide and inspiration.

John reports that even among those who came to him because they were about to be fired by other managers, he saved about half. As for the rest, John says that most of the failing employees left before the deadline, but among those who stayed to the last day the most common parting words were, "Thank you for all you did for me—I know you tried everything."

●

Let's stop and admire what John Opland accomplished: He was saving the majority of employees about to be fired by others. That qualifies not just as a gifted boss, but also as a hero. He is a leader who assumes the best about all the people who work for him; he helps them, and they know it. His employees know exactly where they stand, and where John stands. No mysteries, no intrigue: "Here's the goal and here's where you are now. How do you get from here to there? How can I help?"

●

Now you see why I said before that *what separates de-hiring from firing is that with de-hiring, employees aren't told to leave, but told how to stay.* Employees are offered the chance to make the decision. Many rise up to the challenge and stay, others arrange transfers or find new jobs, and the few who remain at the end of the goal period keep their agreement and leave. Even then, with the last (and smallest) group, it's not the same as being fired. They leave without rancor or animosity because they have had time to understand the situation and have mentally already moved on (already into the job search or career change). No surprises. The gifted boss and the employee are never enemies; they are working together toward an agreement.

Firing is usually preceded by probation (really just a threat) during which the manager looks to confirm the negative feelings that provoked it. With de-hiring, the gifted boss and employee create an agreement and both work toward high expectations. Threat versus agreement. Implicit assumption of failure versus stated assumption of success. Minimum acceptable level of performance versus a new definition of excellence.

●

Assume the best. Help those that want help and those that don't. Assume that everyone has a genius inside and that they'll work hard to prove you right or work hard to get away.

Number 18

The My-Situation-Is-Different Myth: De-Hiring Works in Any Type of Business or Industry, Even Government

The typical manager believes that his or her situation is not typical. However, I have seen de-hiring applied successfully in all types of environments, even where personnel changes are most troublesome.

One manager with a large government agency told me that while civil service regulations make de-hiring more difficult, he has found and used repeatedly a system he calls "sink or swim." He says, "I put overly critical or lethargic people in charge of a sub-project (never a whole project), with an established deadline, a project that has lots of buy-in and a moderate to high profile."

The result, he reports, has been *"to actually change people's work persona,* or *to encourage them to seek a different career path."* The latter has been accomplished, he adds, "without creating any hard enemies."

The genius of this approach is that it's confrontational in a new and positive way—it forces employees to confront themselves and their "work persona." In doing so, this manager rescued employees from mediocrity and saved them from being cast aside, doomed to be given nothing but the least significant projects. He has let them step up or step aside.

●

Here is another look at de-hiring, from Dr. Jonathan Knaupp, a former college professor, who offers us a series of questions:

I have used these in counseling unhappy or disillusioned employees to seek another job. The people I have dealt with over 40 years are mostly college-trained professionals in a school, university, or high-tech industry.

- *Are you happy here? (We already know they are not happy.)*
- *What turns you on, stirs your heart? (In short order, I can get them focused on their desires.)*
- *Does this job do that for you? (Of course not! That's why we are talking.)*
- *How can we make changes so that happens? (Generally, it cannot be done or it is not a problem at work, but rather a personal problem in a relationship or family.)*

- *What would you rather be doing? (They usually already have many ideas about this.)*
- *How can I help you move in that direction? (Often they do not really need specific help, but rather encouragement to make changes.)*

●

In the traditional work environment, employees have to pretend (at least around management) that they love what they do. This lie turns them bitter and nudges them along the downward spiral of doubt and self-pity. The gifted boss breaks through the glass cubicle of happy talk and reminds employees to dream, to move toward their goals, to participate in this overarching goal—every person in the economy doing work they love.

Number 19

Intelligent Failing

Teach educated people to fail intelligently, for failing is one of the greatest arts in the world.
—*Charles Kettering*

●

When people hang on, doing mediocre work, they require your leadership to help them let go and start anew. *In failure is freedom.*

●

I wish I could assert that de-hiring is always a simple matter—just asking, "Are you happy?" or setting a few goals, standing back, and seeing what happens. There are times when people can't or won't succeed, and moreover, can't or won't leave.

"Steve" is the director of development for a private school, and tells us of the time he inherited an employee, "Artie," who was bored, openly unhappy in his job, a drag on the department, but who, nevertheless, was leaning on Steve for a major promotion. Far from wanting to promote Artie, Steve had determined that Artie was not going to rise to the challenge of being a star, at least not in Steve's system, and he urged Artie to apply for jobs at other schools. Let's listen to Steve's description of what transpired:

About a month after the conversation in which I urged him to look elsewhere, a member of our staff announced she would be leaving to stay home with her kids. Artie met with me to say he would love that job. He seemed to expect I would give it to him, despite our earlier conversations. I told him that he could apply, but I repeated to him that since he hated his current job, he should actively seek challenges at other schools. I advised him not to put all his eggs in one basket (at our school). I told him I would help him. I would be a reference. The next day, I put some job ads in his mailbox that I thought would be interesting to him.

Artie came into my office the next day, after receiving the job ads, and said with tears in his eyes that he didn't want to go somewhere else. I listened. I was sympathetic. I felt badly for him, I really did. But I stayed on course and repeated my previous advice.

Unbeknownst to me, he applied for one of the jobs that I had given to him. And he got an offer. He came to me to tell me he had this offer and was hoping I would beg him to stay. I congratulated him on the offer and urged him to take it. It was a raise of about 20 percent. It was an increase of responsibility of about 200 percent. It was a major step forward in his career. He should take it. He listened, then went and wrote an e-mail to the head of the school telling him about the offer and asking for a meeting. He agreed to meet with Artie, but invited me to come, too—the head of the school and I were on the same page in this whole process.

The head of the school encouraged Artie to take the job. Artie teared up. He wanted to stay. We wanted him to go.

Artie took the job. He saved face. He got a promotion. And we replaced this weak employee with a star. I am struck by the fact that our office improved dramatically through this process because of two separate things: (1) We subtracted a bad employee who hurt team morale, made a lot of mistakes, complained, and so on. (2) We added a star employee who helped morale, is a perfectionist, is cheerful and reliable, and so on. I feel like we got a double-bonus even though this involved only one position.

I like to think that if Steve had had the benefit of everything we know about de-hiring, he might have been able to find a way to save his weak employee, or, if nothing else, get him to see that he wasn't going to rise up to Steve's expectations and come to terms with that fact, without tears or resentments. Beyond any second-guessing, though, we can appreciate Steve's victory—getting an employee to leave, and doing so in a way that propelled that man's career forward not back. Steve advanced Artie's career in more ways than one, and I suspect that one fine day Artie will recognize it, and be grateful to Steve, perhaps even find ways to help him.

I include Steve's story here because we may encounter employees who "don't get it," who refuse to succeed or to leave. I hope you never have to start an employee's job search, like Steve did, but I'm certain Steve would agree that each hour he spent finding job ads for his weak employee saved him a thousand hours of managing, trying to overcome that employee's shortcomings, and repairing damage to the team's morale.

Number 20

You Can't Buy Love from Fired Employees

You might wonder, Why fritter away all that time with de-hiring when you can just fire struggling employees, then soften the blow with the time or severance to let them find something else?

Here's a story from early in my entrepreneurial days, illustrating how badly it can go when you decide you're going to fire someone while being nice and generous.

I used to own a market research consulting company. I was *not* a gifted boss—that's why I started researching them, because I was envious of how easy it seemed to be for some leaders. Still, my company was a thriving business thanks to my exhausting personal efforts at managing the staff, and, much more important, having a tidy little research niche that brought us major corporate clients. I decided to hire another senior person to be the new head of marketing, something I'd been doing along with my other duties as owner.

I made a classic hiring mistake—hiring a friend who'd been fired. After many frustrating months without any progress, I sat down with him for the it's-not-working-out talk. In another classic mistake, I assumed that it was obvious that it wasn't working out, but he was surprised. The upshot was a series of tense conversations; after all, he was a friend, and having just been fired from a bigger firm, he believed that he couldn't find a new job having been fired again so soon. So, he asked that he remain on the payroll for three months, during which time he would continue to do marketing, but take time off for interviews. It seemed reasonable. Yet another mistake, of course.

Those three months ruined the friendship, as he didn't find a new job and became resentful. I had my own resentments: He was flying around the country, doing job-search networking and charging it to my company as "sales trips." Finally, the last day of his last month, I asked him to lunch to discuss what we'd tell people, and so forth. There at the restaurant, he declared, "I've decided I'm not leaving."

He'd consulted an attorney and suddenly felt he was entitled to much more, based on our old discussions about how good it could have been. I was adamant, and he left. I never heard from him or his attorney. However, even now, more than two decades later, I feel my stomach knot when recalling that day. As you can imagine, this experience spurred my interest in becoming one of those laughing managers who handled employment situations effortlessly.

●

What brought back to mind that personal management failure was hearing from Ed Leighton, who spent five years as an outplacement counselor. I pass along a bit of his wisdom:

I met hundreds of individuals who had been downsized, right-sized, or whatever, and not one of them was happy about being rejected, no matter how obviously righteous (objectively speaking) the decision was. And company generosity did nothing to assuage the pain. If anything, it only served to delay the real need to learn a lesson from the experience, then get back on the horse.

From a psychological perspective, no one wants to be sold. They prefer to make a conscious choice to buy. In other words, being asked to leave is rejection, no matter how you dress it up. Even if the candidate knows the company was in the right, their ego will not permit them to accept that reality. Each and every one of them would have preferred a face-saving resignation, yet rarely do such candidates take that initiative. I had one guy confess to me (sadly) that he survived by keeping his head down and hoping no one noticed how dumb he was. One day someone did.

My outplacement employer was fond of saying (in confidence), "We get all the rejects." Of course, he was referring to the obvious [that they'd just been rejected]. But he also meant that those who get let go are usually those who brought a life of unresolved issues into the job. Eventually those qualities caught up with them.

I'm sure there are outplacement people who read those words and take umbrage, who might even accuse Ed of bitterness or overstatement. Yes, there certainly are terrific employees who get caught up in layoffs. Even so, we should consider Ed's contention that being asked to leave is rejection "no matter how you dress it up" and that "generosity did nothing to assuage the pain," just postponed the lesson that needed to be learned. I think there's an important tough-love message in that.

Let's think together about an employer who is firing an employee but who decides, "I don't want to burn any bridges." Is that possible? All we have to do is look at "firing" and see its root "fire" lurking there. *Firing is "burning."* You can dress it up, but it's still rejection. Say the company decides to be generous and gives the employee a year of pay and benefits. There's a good chance that the employee will take a few months off, taking a "much deserved break." Meanwhile, his industry knowledge is eroding, and when he does start looking, he'll have to explain why it's taken him so long to find a job. (He can say he took a break, but most hiring managers assume the worst; namely, other hiring managers have passed on him. If nothing else, what does it say about your passion for work if you haven't been working? Are you *burned* out?) In other words, what seems like generosity might, in fact, be its opposite.

As for the rejection, dressed up or not, it has to hurt the fired employee's self-esteem. It could even be that the more you pay someone to leave, the more their self-esteem is hurt—They paid all that money just to get rid of me?

The solution is to use layoffs only in extremes of financial desperation and to use firing in definitive cases of "fired for cause." The latter being cases where the employee has violated the company's trust, where an abrupt firing is important and can increase loyalty and morale. In every other case, the de-hiring process is cheaper, easier, and kinder.

Number 21

From Set-Up-to-Fail to Set-Up-to-Be-a-Hero

The same logic of the de-hiring process—assuming the best, establishing goals for success and stardom, working with the employee to reach those goals—is the logic of leadership, in general. What if you had a de-hiring conversation *before* the employee started struggling, maybe even before the employee started working for you? It might look like this:

It's a companywide managers' meeting for a chain of lumberyards. The head of the management information department has been hearing complaints and suggestions for 20 minutes. That's when one of the managers stands up and says, "We've been complaining, but I want you to know that we appreciate all you've done for us." The group starts applauding and then rises for a spontaneous standing ovation.

That standing ovation was four years in the making, for it was four years prior that Dan Fesler, the CEO of Lampert Yards, hired a new head of information systems, and when he did, he confided to his new employee, "Half the people here hate your department." He then added, "Can we set it up so everybody likes you? If so, you'll accomplish twice as much." Together, they worked out a plan. They decided that the animosity derived from the company's managers only thinking about the computer system when something didn't work or when they couldn't get data. So, Dan and his new director decided that they would get the managers to help create a prioritized list of what improvements were needed; then, each month, the manager's meeting would include an update on progress against that list.

You can see how attitudes were subtly shifted—instead of focusing only on what was wrong or missing, the managers started to see and appreciate the improvements taking place. The result was that, instead of being disliked and mistrusted, the people in management information became allies and then heroes.

●

Compare that experience to the process described in the important book *The Set-Up-to-Fail Syndrome* by Manzoni and Barsoux:

The set-up-to-fail syndrome begins innocuously enough. The triggering event could be specific — perhaps an employee misses a target or a deadline, loses a client, or gives a poor report or presentation. The trigger could also be quite vague — maybe the employee arrived from another unit with a lukewarm recommendation or reacted oddly to early advice from the boss. In any case, something sows a doubt in the boss's mind.

You know what happens next — more supervision, more checking up. Sometimes this works — the employee welcomes the oversight and performance improves. But the syndrome Manzoni and Barsoux observed was just the opposite — the employees' performance declined due to self-doubts or resistance to the managerial interference. When the latter happens, how do managers respond? By increasing the supervision, and thus greasing the downward spiral. Moreover, there is a "confirmatory bias," which is another way of saying that we tend to see what we expect to see — in this case, performance shortcomings or negative attitudes.

●

With the set-up-to-fail syndrome as background, let's reconsider Dan Fesler of Lampert Yards. He said of his experience with information systems, "I was bringing an employee into an ugly situation and I wanted to find a way to turn it into an opportunity to be a hero." So, it would be fair to say that Fesler created the opposite of a set-up-to-fail syndrome; he created a set-up-to-be-a-hero syndrome.

Number 22

You Aren't Just Changing Employees—You're Changing Lives

Gifted bosses don't manage; they create "circles of helping." They want what is best for everyone, but as you know, figuring out what's truly best is often problematic. Given the compassion and humility of how GEO bosses tend their "circles," it didn't surprise me to learn that some of them turn to a higher power as the ultimate business consultant. One of those most open about her workplace prayers is Lila Woodword—now retired after holding a series of leadership positions, starting at a time when women were largely excluded from such jobs.

She says of her hiring decisions, "I would always ask the Lord to make it clear to me which one man or woman was His choice for the position. And one person would always stand out above the others."

She adds, "I still hear from many of them, even the ones I hired thirty years ago."

This system worked so well that Lila could recall only two employees in her long career whose hiring she regretted. Her solution to those exceptions? She said:

I prayed about it. I'd say, "Lord I have this one man who doesn't fit in with the rest. What should I do?" And I knew that I shouldn't criticize. Instead, I always tried to focus on the person's need to follow his God-given talents and qualities into another area. One young man was an outstanding guitarist, and I went to him and said, "I think you would be happier pursuing your musical gifts." And he smiled and said, "You know, Lila, I've been thinking that myself. I'm going to take your advice" The other man's father owned a restaurant and I suggested that his father needed him and that he should go and help, and he said, "I think you're right. Thank you."

•

I mention Lila's experience to invite you to admire the seriousness with which some leaders approach their organizational husbandry. They understand that their decisions alter the course of lives while testing their own characters. Does it help to pray about hiring decisions? How could it not? Consulting a higher power can only elevate the mental conversation, activate the part of the mind that is most kind, most loving, most likely to find a way to help, most likely to connect with the other person at the level of respect and compassion, and to invite into the circle of helping what Lincoln called the "better angels of our nature."

Number 23

Lessons from a Master of the Art of De-Hiring

Let's pull together what we've learned about the de-hiring process by way of an example. Of all the gifted bosses I've studied, the one who has most completely developed and analyzed the process of de-hiring is a financial executive in Chicago, Mike McLaughlin. He has become so skilled at gracefully moving along nonstar employees that his friends have come to call his process "The McLaughlin Method."

Mike has spent over three decades working with financial organizations, especially working with actuaries, both as a consultant and in corporations, and currently works for a large consulting firm, heading a department with worldwide responsibilities. It seems fitting that a man who came up as an actuary, assessing risk and probabilities, would have worked out his own system for spotting the life expectancy of skills and talents.

I. The Wisdom of Honest Assessment

Mike explains his attitude toward employees who are underperforming:

If you have a person who is missing deadlines or making mistakes, the first thing is to tell them so. You have to communicate that their performance is bad, and that means saying that it's bad. Some people use cliches like "not reaching full potential." That's a disservice. It's not a clear enough message.

●

II. The Quantifiable Improvement Period

McLaughlin follows the assessment conversation with a process that he calls "turning up the heat." He quickly added, "This is not meant to bully the person, but to focus them. You *cannot* do it in a way that the person is doomed to fail. A *fundamental requirement is that they have a fair chance to succeed.*" He also offered this caveat: "What could happen in theory—although it's never happened to me—is that the person feels discriminated against. So don't bully. You can't put higher goals on the one person than others in similar jobs."

(I personally would not use the expression "turning up the heat," fearing a negative connotation if employees overhear the phrase. We are, after all, pursuing a no-secrets style of leadership. So, I would call it "the quantifiable improvement period," "turnaround time," "goal period," or "challenge timetable." But back to Mike's system. . . .)

He establishes, formally, a turnaround agreement. The timetable might be 30, 60, or 90 days, maybe as long as six months—depending on the person and the level. It's long enough to give the person time to improve, or time to decide to pursue some other position. But it isn't just time: The key to making de-hiring work is to have a way to quantify shortcomings and successes, so all that we soon learn about pay-for-performance comes into play. In McLaughlin's case, he says, "You work out what improvement means. It might be three or four projects on deadline. Or if it's something like 'better relationship with accounting,' you add, 'as evidenced by 10 invoices approved on first go round.'"

•

III. The Three Outcomes

No Improvement

The rarest of the three possible results is that the improvement period ends without the desired achievements, and the employee leaves (keeping up his or her end of the agreement) or is fired. However, by giving the employee a chance, you've accomplished something for the person and the organization: Mike, a veteran of large corporations, puts it, "Human resources wants documentation and you have it." More important, you have given employees the chance to encounter the hard truth that they are in the wrong place, and you have forced them to think about what will come next: As Mike says:

When the person is in the wrong job, they know. Typically, they are, at some level, almost hoping to be fired. I had a recent case where I started a new job and inherited an underperformer. He knew it, and he was under stress, but no one had fired him. The other managers had just let him slide. So, I gave him an easy project, one where he could succeed and start to build his confidence back. But he didn't do it. So, I fired him. I heard through the grapevine that he was relieved. And I think that's a test of the system—How does the person feel afterward?

●

The Turnaround Succeeds

A common outcome of the quantifiable improvement period is that the underperformer rises up to expectations and becomes a solid contributor. How often does this happen? Mike's experience suggests that "miracles"—where the employee goes from being a poor performer to a star—are rare, but that rising "to expectations" is common.

Having had the chance to study hundreds of de-hirings, I have found the miracles to which Mike refers. I've concluded that the de-hiring situation in which this is most likely is when the person doesn't just change attitude, but changes something fundamental about the work or work environment—the case of the second-rate manager who became a star analyst, or the salesperson who became a star technician. There are, moreover, cases where the de-hiring process awakened something in the person, and he or she was able to hitch onto an upward spiral—a small victory at work, learning, greater confidence, bigger victory with more learning, even greater confidence, and so on—until the struggling employee is remade into a star.

The Person Self-Selects out of the Job

The other common result of the turnaround period is that the employee resigns. In Mike's words:

The employees think "It's not a good fit" or "The expectations are too high" and say to themselves, "It's not as much fun anymore." Sometimes these are people who are able to meet the expectations, but it required such enormous effort that they self-select out.

●

So, fitting the pieces together, what do we have? The HR people are happy—Mike reports having gotten thank-you calls from the personnel people who were saved from a trying intervention. The former employee is nearly always better off, usually looking back with relief or gratitude. And just as the employee is not diminished by the experience, so the leader has not been diminished, has not failed, but has succeeded in helping an employee find a place to be a star. The team is relieved, because the de-hired person was clearly struggling. And lastly, a stronger contributor can be hired, enabling the team to generate more victories.

Let's end with one last point from Mike, and it's a beauty, about the ethics of the de-hiring process:

The temptation when you have an underperformer is to wait and wait, but what's the result? When that person eventually leaves, they are three or five years older [years spent learning how to live with being second-rate], and their options have narrowed. It's your duty to de-hire sooner rather than later.

Part IV
great
EMPLOYEES ONLY

Inspiring, Effortless
Leadership (The First Step
in Hiring Great Employees)

Number 24

You Can Take Credit, but You Can't Give It Away

When I do seminars on leadership, I sometimes talk about Lou Holtz (the former football coach who won a National Championship at Notre Dame) and how during our interview he proudly enumerated the assistant coaches he'd helped become head coaches at other colleges. And by "helping," I don't just mean giving them the visibility of a major program and then not interfering when they left; no, I mean he would *actively sell them* to athletic directors at other schools. This is a startling notion to some of the managers I speak to—ones who came to the seminar to learn how to eliminate turnover. Then I point out that Lou Holtz kept a list—it was then a *secret* list—of people he wanted to hire. He'd hear of young coaches with exceptional talent and arrange to meet them at a coaches' conference. He'd interview them without their knowing it, and decide if they were worthy of The List.

So, when it came time to help his assistants land great jobs, he wasn't just losing a great employee, he was moving on to the next star employee, to the next source of ideas and energy. He had *The List*.

This is where some managers object, saying that Lou Holtz was famous and at a famous football school, so that he had his choice of people to hire. True enough. But then again, *part of the reason he got to be a famous coach at a famous football school was because he had great assistants, and he had great assistants because he had a history of helping them move up*. Working for a legend was appealing, but when the legend was also a conduit for moving ahead, the most ambitious and hardworking assistants were eager to sign on. However, you don't have to be famous to develop a reputation for helping assistants advance.

That brings us back to David Rains, the PetSmart store manager. Remember that I sought out David because of his reputation within PetSmart as a star at hiring great people. How did he earn that reputation? As David put it, "Some people get a bit selfish, trying to hold onto employees, but I like to see people who worked for me get promoted." He then fell into telling me about his colleagues, who'd gone on to terrific new jobs, including one who was now a fellow store manager, sounding a bit like Lou Holtz.

What I also like about David Rains's example is that he brings together two notions, at either end of the hiring spectrum: On one hand, as we saw earlier, he helps employees who might leave PetSmart if not for him, including some who are struggling elsewhere. On the other hand, he helps the best employees get promoted, even if it means they leave his store. In both cases, he builds the reputations of those who work for him, and in doing so, he has built a reputation for hiring and for a terrific staff. Assume the best and it comes back to you. Giving credit is credit worthy.

The first step in inspiring people is to make it clear that they will get credit, along with your help in advancing in their careers. You aren't managing them—you are inviting them to be lifelong allies.

Grab credit, it runs away. Give it away; it returns even as you're giving it. You can give away a car that doesn't run; you can give away old clothes; you can even give away fruitcake; but you can't give away credit.

Number 25

Effortless Leadership, Part I: No One Wants to Be Managed, so *Stop Doing It*

Management is boring. To be managed is to be held back, held down, controlled, watched, trained, and instructed. Look up *manage* in ThinkMap's visual thesaurus and you find such dreariness as *supervise, grapple, make do, cope, wangle, finagle, oversee* and *get by*. Which of those will make you want to get out of bed? Which will make your employees look forward to seeing you?

However, look up *inspire* and you find: *revolutionize, urge on, invigorate, enliven, animate, exhort* and *cheer*. Now *that's* a boss you want to see, to share ideas with, to triumph with.

The best managers work at not managing. What great bosses understand is what we learned at the very start—leadership success is:

A: 90 percent hiring and de-hiring,
B: 10 percent inspiring, and
C: 0 percent managing (if an employee can't be inspired and needs managing, see A.)

Number 26

Effortless Leadership, Part II: Management by Asking Questions

If you believe that work is one of three pillars in life, along with family and community/spiritual involvement, you have an obligation to yourself to find interesting work; further, as a boss, you are called to help employees find meaningful and rewarding work, whether it's with you or not. This often means de-hiring, but sometimes it only means asking a few tough questions.

Don Urbanciz is an insurance executive in Chicago, and a gifted boss. One of his employees, "Karen," was obviously unhappy in her job. Most managers would avoid that person, not wanting to hear complaints, or simply fire her. Don, however, invited this employee out for coffee. Their conversation boiled down to something like this:

Don: You're miserable. What's wrong?
Karen: I hate my job. I loathe coming to work.
Don: What would change that?
Karen: My job is a waste of time. What I do could be done by a computer.

First, we have to recognize Don Urbanciz for being the sort of boss that an employee could confess to about being miserable, and give Karen credit for not just honesty but vision. Don didn't transfer her, but instead assigned her to experiment with automating the process that she and two coworkers were doing by hand. She quickly figured out how to eliminate three boring jobs. Soon, she was traveling to the company's other offices, showing them how to do it.

The other employees were reassigned, and as for the miserable employee, Don says he knew he'd made the right decision the day another executive referred to the formerly glum employee by saying, "Hey, what happened? She said 'hello' to me today."

Why doesn't this happen more often? Don has an answer:

Most managers are afraid to ask because of what they'll hear and how they won't know how to deal with it: They assume they're going to just hear complaints—"I'm not paid enough" or "I work too many

*hours." It's easier to put them on probation and 90
days later get rid of them.*

•

There's no energy in closure; the action is in
aperture. Inspiration arises from the same conversation as de-hiring, allowing us to see what can be accomplished by rehiring an employee into a new role.

Number 27

Effortless Leadership, Part III: The One Who Manages Least, Manages Best

The owner of the Phoenix Rock Gym, Paul Diefenderfer, is proud that he looks like a hippie—proud to wear his hair in a ponytail, flash a peace sign, or tell you how he doesn't own a tie. But he really got my attention when he said something startling, coming as it did from an entrepreneur: "My official day is Wednesday—I'm always here on Wednesdays."

This led to a long talk with Paul about his business methods. I then went back through our discussion, pulled out topics, and put them together by subject. The result is a tidy philosophy, worth reading because it's a system of anti-management leadership, and, as we soon see, it creates a culture that does the hiring and de-hiring:

●

The Hippie's Guide to Business

Hippie Marketing

- *A lot of rock gyms opened on the health club model, where they just want to get you to sign a contract and get your automatic payment started. They try to upgrade you and upgrade you—you want to take a shower, not from working out but from talking to the salespeople. Here, if you want a day pass—great. You want a month—fine. If you're buying so many day passes that you'd be better off with a monthly, we'll point that out; but that's all. No contracts. No pressure. We want to be like the bar "Cheers," where you feel at home and "everyone knows your name."*

Hippie Finance

- *My friend and I each put in ten grand. I'm pretty handy, so I built the walls and put in the electrical. We never had any debt. Later, I bought out my partner and bought a building to move into. Still, no debt, just the mortgage on the building, and the building is my retirement.*

Hippie Competitiveness

- *We were the first rock gym in the state and when a couple of others opened up, I thought, "Ah, man,*

*that's messin' me up." Then I thought, "No, it's
going to make us better." Business is like climbing:
You CANNOT SIT.*

- *One way we get better is to have the best route set-
ters around—one full-time and one part-time. It's
an art form. Anybody can make it hard; the art is
to make it INTERESTING.*

Hippie Management

- *I don't set schedules. The calendar is open and people sign up. We tend to have the most business on
weekends, and that's when a lot of people want
time off. So, the pay goes up by a dollar an hour
on weekends.*
- *The days when the fewest employees sign up
are holidays. So, I work those, so staff can have
them off.*
- *We have a bonus pool, based on revenues. I
want them to know that if we're busy, they make
more. And I want them to understand that I
just pass money along, from the customers to them.
I always say to the employees, "I don't pay you, I
just transfer money from the customers to you."*

●

Rereading those sentiments, it's easy to see why
Paul has so much free time: He has simply opted
out of the tasks that occupy so much of other managers' time.

Let's take a look at how a typical control-oriented boss handles one common management task—employee scheduling. A homebuilder got a new sales manager; let's call him "Sean." He joined an office where the sales agents had been doing their own work schedules, accepting responsibility for figuring out the busiest days and making sure the model homes were staffed.

The process was informal but effective: One of the agents would draft a preliminary schedule, then the other agents shuffled days, happy to help coworkers, knowing that their cooperation would be repaid. It worked so smoothly that no one thought to question the procedure. However, Sean needed control and declared that he alone would create a monthly schedule. Sometimes, he'd be slow to getting to it, frustrating the agents who had outside lives to plan. Before Sean, any employee could initiate the scheduling process—"I'm planning a vacation for next month so can we do the schedule so I can buy my airline tickets?" Not now. They could only ask each other, "Has Sean done the schedule?" Once it was completed and distributed, if something came up, you could arrange to trade with someone else, but you had to check with Sean. If he was out of town, you might not get his okay for days.

Sean spent hours a month on scheduling, and what thanks did he get? None. The staff would often

(continued)

(Continued)

grumble about schedules and blame Sean when they were under- or overstaffed. Before, they had no one to blame but themselves; Sean changed that.

In that example, we see the insidious nature of bureaucracy, spending hours to do something less well than if it were done by those directly involved. It's negative work, yielding negative energy and negative morale.

The Parting Shot versus the Parting Gift

There's one last item I saved from the "hippie" summary, because I wanted it to stand alone, to let us savor it together, and that topic is how Paul handles de-hiring. He says about underperforming employees, with a shrug, "Sometimes it doesn't work out. If there's a problem, I sit down with the employee and say, 'Here's what I'm hearing. How can I help you do better?'"

That should sound familiar—the classic good-hearted boss, working to help, willing to experiment. However, if the employee is not eager to do better, then Paul says, "'You can be happy working here, or not. If not, then no hard feelings. No big deal. Be happy.' Then I'll give them a free month pass as a parting gift and say, 'We'll be friends.' And we are."

Isn't that marvelous? This is the only case I've encountered where a boss gives a de-hired employee a
parting gift. Most bosses, without meaning to, get in
a parting shot—the empty box for belongings, along
with the security escort or a third person in the room
as a witness. The typical manager offers up blows to
the self-esteem that do irreparable harm to the relationship. Not Paul.

The result is that he has *rehired many of his employees.* He says:

*We do have a couple of firing offenses. For instance, if
you do not show up for work twice, you have lost your
job. Period. One employee, after the second time, said
to me, "But I love my job." I said, "No you don't. If you
loved it, you would have been here."*

This was said simply, without rancor or moral
topspin. Then, Paul gave him the gift and said sin-
cerely that he hoped he'd see him in the gym and
that they would stay friends.

Paul did indeed see the young man in the
gym, who on one occasion he ventured, "I sure do
miss working here." Paul smiled and said, "If I were
you, I'd re-apply and see what happens." Paul hired
him again and says, "I'd much rather rehire someone—they know the place and don't need to be
trained. And he's been terrific. A great employee,
and he's never been late, much less missed a day,
ever since."

Now *that's* classic GEO-boss thinking. You don't need to prove yourself right, much less prove someone else wrong. There's no blaming, no arguing, just an agreement to be kept, and the creation of an opportunity to let someone learn and rise up to a new, better self.

Number 28

Effortless Leadership, Part IV: Winning versus Working

The best employees want to *manage themselves,* and the GEO boss is eager to let them. However, self-management is still management, and what are the essential, effective tools of managing? They aren't bagels or posters, much less nagging or mothering. They are the scorecard, the dashboard, the stats, the data—in other words, the numbers that tell you how you're doing. If you want people to self-manage, you have to give them the data to know when they are succeeding. Let's look at how quickly and easily a GEO boss can implement the essence of such a system, and then take a longer look at how a self-managing system can be fully realized:

•

When [employees] get home, what do they say about their day at work? Do they go home happy? Isn't that what we want for the people we care about? If we really care about employees, don't we want it for them?

— Bob Chapman, CEO of Barry-Wehmiller of St. Louis, world leader in packaging equipment

Notice in that quote how Bob Chapman is broadening leadership, acknowledging that gifted bosses think in terms of employees' lives, and they help make lives better with leadership, creating systems that lead to self-managing employees.

Bob told me about the time he visited a subsidiary they'd recently acquired: "I met with the customer service employees and asked them, 'How do you know if you're doing a good job?' One said, 'If only a couple of customers yell at me, then it's a good day.'"

What Bob understood is that if avoiding getting yelled at is the goal, what's the best way to reach it? To take as few calls as possible. Further, even when the customers were not yelling, each call represented possible problems. As one employee confided, "A big order is a lot of work."

Bob responded by creating a game. It was simple and direct—a small cash prize was given to whoever sold the most parts, as well as prizes to any team that exceeded its goal. The results were immediate and profound—people started helping one another and started winning. He says of that experience:

All I wanted was to get people to want to pick up the phone, and then to have a chance to go home feeling they'd won. I didn't plan it to increase sales, but it happened anyway—revenues went up nearly 30 percent by the end of that quarter.

●

Now, let's look at another Barry-Wehmiller company and see how Bob Chapman's inspiration is guiding a program . . . without his being involved in the day-to-day operations.

That other Barry-Wehmiller company is MarquipWardUnited, in Baltimore. It's a company that has undertaken a "Lean" program, as inspired by Toyota, but imbued with Bob Chapman's humanistic approach to leadership. The result has been to make jobs more rewarding while making them more productive.

The folks at MarquipWardUnited seek to understand work at a deeper level. One way to do this is to videotape people working. I know, I know—this has a creepy, Big-Brotherish feel to it; however, that's where the trust inspired by their CEO's leadership comes into play. The idea is not to second-guess how the individual works, but to allow the employee and others, including those who know nothing of the specific job, to see it through fresh eyes. I'm told that the most useful question in these sessions is, "Why do you do it that way?" Tadgh Prendeville, one of the plant's team leaders, says, "When someone answers that question with 'We've always done it that way,' then we know we're onto something."

The result of these sessions, when done properly, is that people begin to think of their work in new ways. For one thing, their work is worthy of examination and discussion, rather like television analysts breaking down the work of politicians or athletes. And because employees are involved with others from the business, they start to see how their efforts fit into the flow of work for the larger operation. Tadgh says that people end up seeing their work as more important and often say, "I'm getting more done" and taking that further to, "My life got better."

But there's another reason to analyze each job, and that's to define success. Because their CEO wants everyone to know if they've had a good day, it means coming up with a way to win, which means coming up with measurements.

Kendrick "Kip" Brennan of MarquipWardUnited explained to me how it works, using one of the nontechnical functions:

At one point, we discovered we had a three-month backlog in accounts payable. We found that the backlog was because of entering invoices in the accounts payable system. There was a desk with invoices stacked a foot and a half high. How many invoices needed to be processed a day to catch up? No one knew.

We wanted a simple visual system that would let people know if they were winning or not. So, we did some calculations, then attached a series of plastic holders on a board, one for each day of the week, and each one with the right number of invoices that needed to be entered in a day. We knew that if a holder got emptied each day, then we'd catch up in a few weeks. But it turned out that once the process was laid out, the backlog was cleared in two weeks.

Before, the people in accounts payable always felt like they were behind, like they were losing. So, knowing what needed to be done relieved stress. Now they know when they have a victory, just like they know, well in advance, if they need to make a correction in their process.

Looking more broadly, there was another benefit, as set out by Tadgh Preneville:

Everyone in accounts payable started to see how every job fit into the flow. They know the importance of entering the invoices. If they don't get entered, then suppliers start to call wondering what happened, and ultimately they can hold shipments because an old invoice hasn't been paid. So, employees understand their jobs in context. And because of that under-standing, it's no longer just one person responsible for getting invoices into the system; now, others pitch in to help. They are cross-training each other so they can help one another. It's no longer a person who just enters invoices every day for thirty years. Now the work is worthwhile.

Did you notice that beautiful little statement, "They are cross-training each other"? When manage-ment stops managing and starts inspiring, employees find ways to make work better and figure out how to help one another. They learn, grow, and win. Manage-ment doesn't impose ideas, just a great scoring system. To truly make employees self-managing, all we need to do next is tie the work and compensation together. Once you create the game and start having wins and losses, it's a simple matter to tie bonuses to victory and make the game that much more motivating and ener-gizing. Employees go home happy because they won and did it themselves, without being managed.

The folks at MarquipWardUnited have created a work environment so impressive that their customers have taken note. Customers ask to be trained in the company's methods and pay to become the company's students. This includes among other things, working on the shop floor. Thus, as Rhonda Spencer, director of organizational empowerment, put it, "They are paying us to clean our machines." That's the power of true leadership, of believing in shared happiness and offering a vision of a more satisfying way of working. While people avoid management, they seek out inspiration.

Number 29

Guess What Kind of Employee Is Attracted to Average Pay?

My friend Dr. Richard Gooding is a consultant specializing in helping rapidly growing organizations. Richard tells me that the book *Good to Great* is popular with executives trying to keep up with growth and that there's one principle more helpful than any other: "First who, then what." *Good to Great* author Jim Collins puts it this way:

We expected that good-to-great leaders would begin by setting a new vision and strategy. We found instead that they first got the right people on the bus, the wrong people off the bus, and the right people in the right seats—and then they figured out where to drive it.

If you hear businesspeople talking about "the bus," odds are they're talking about steering the business, not getting home.

Richard says, "You get the right 'who' and running the company becomes easy. Get the right people and problems actually *get fixed!* The company becomes fun and exciting." Which takes us back to the twin sisters of excellence—hiring and de-hiring. Most bosses understand the need for star employees; ask any headhunter and he or she will tell you that every manager specifies a "star." But there's a problem with hiring stars: Why shouldn't an exceptional performer be earning substantially more than the ordinary performer? Yet, that's not how most budgets work. Most companies have built a perpetual mediocrity machine.

In most large organizations, the folks in human resources do a compensation survey, which means finding out what other companies are paying, then establish a salary range. The manager hopes to hire someone below the top of that range, to allow room for raises. Said another way, the company wants to hire in the middle of the range, which is the average salary for the job/industry. And in the long run, when you offer average pay, you get average people doing average work.

Richard Gooding offers us this example, from one of his clients, a company that was yearning to get their products into the "big box" retailers. Their national accounts salesperson was working hard, earning his $60 thousand a year by bringing in $300 thousand in business. They found a new salesperson, who cost $120 thousand, but who brought in $2 million in sales his first year. Which employee is cheap and which one is expensive?

It's when we move outside of sales that the justification of high salaries becomes more difficult as the output becomes harder to measure. When I devoted one of my newspaper columns to the notion of pay-for-performance, I received many responses from frustrated and cautious HR people, typified by this one:

My only question is, will you be there when the Equal Employment Opportunity Commission (EEOC) knocks on the door and asks to review salary records? Will you be willing to be the one to explain why there are discrepancies in pay rates? There are reasons why HR professionals work diligently to maintain internal equity and articles like these make our jobs that much more difficult! We work very hard to treat our employees fairly and equitably and to comply with state and federal regulations so the risk of formal complaints is minimized. . . . Employees just don't understand, or don't want to understand, that there are limits as to what we can pay!

So you see what you're up against in creating a pay-for-performance system. And here's the result, as stated by a star employee who read the same column:

My company has "rules" that limit raises, which aren't based on performance. I'm in purchasing at my company. In my first year, I saved 8 times my salary. In my second, 13.5 times my salary. Both my raise and bonus were exactly the same each time. My third year I saved 21.5 times my salary—and got no bonus at all! Will I remain "loyal" in the long term? I'd have to be an idiot.

●

The best people in HR are those who understand the mind of the star employee and seek to find ways to reward that person. Otherwise, the best people leave, and the second-rate ones, the ones with the fewest employment options, don't—all fuel for the perpetual mediocrity machine. If you can find an ally in HR, one of the people who "gets it," then you can start to undo the fear that leads to averages-based hiring policies. If not, you are going to have to find ways to reward performance and let stars be stars.

Number 30

Never Bet on Employees Who Don't Want to Bet on Themselves

You can't "manage" people. But you can bribe them.
— David Aycock

●

Pamela Mix is one of those people in HR who gets it; she understands that HR people can be more than policy police, that they can become major contributors to productivity and to acquiring and retaining top talent. Mix is the vice president for human resources at the College of American Pathologists and here's how she talks about her group's efforts to move toward rewarding performance:

We rolled out a broad pay-for-performance effort last year. It has three components, all to be aligned with performance: base pay, annual incentive (bonus), and special recognition. In addition to the compensation systems themselves, we've been doing extensive management training, both on how to use the compensation systems (managers are responsible for pay decisions), and especially on performance management skills (goal setting, feedback, retention, etc.) As you might imagine, **there is a wide range of competence among managers, and a pretty good correlation (anecdotally) between the manager's performance management skills and the degree of differentiation he or she makes in allocating rewards.** *We're seeing improvement, though.*

Having worked with pay for performance in several organizations, I might point out that not all employees like pay for performance. In an organization with a paternalistic culture and an entrenched entitlement mentality, many people would prefer to all get the same rewards (preferably as high as possible!) **Not surprisingly, these are many of the same people who are not getting the highest rewards in a pay-for-performance system.** *The compensation system puts a spotlight on performance and holds people accountable. This is highly desirable for the organization, but the transition can be difficult for individuals.*

●

If you took note of the bold items, you see the pattern—the best managers are best at rewarding performance, and the worst employees hate pay-for-performance. In other words, it is a system that, by its very presence, begins to sort out the bureaucrats from the players. The game is rigged in your favor because you know what kind of workers you have by watching who wants to play. Never bet on people who don't want to bet on themselves.

Number 31

What's the Score?
or
How to Go from
Shooting Around to
Playing to Win

Pay, especially the bonus, is a scorecard. If you have ambitious, competitive people, they want to turn the numbers over on the board. It's not just greed, but competitive zeal. Take, for instance, the leverage gained in how you divvy up the bonus payments, as demonstrated with this case study from PetSmart.

When the price of PetSmart's stock fell from nearly $30 a share to below $3, the leadership team was forced to reconsider their strategy, especially how to compete with Wal-Mart. They realized that their system had been built around distribution not the customer. The result was, in the words of president Robert Moran, "a new vision, given to us by our customers."

When Moran did a program at the Services Leadership Conference, he asked the audience how

many people had a dog or cat. Nearly all the hands
went up. Then he asked how many had bought their
pet a gift in the last few months. About one-third.
And then he asked, "How many of you, when talking
about your pets at home, call yourself Mommy or
Daddy?" This produced an odd noise, a combination
of embarrassed chuckling and a gasp of being found
out. No hands went up, but most of the faces told the
story—yes, we are Mommy and Daddy. And so
being, we are part of PetSmart's new target market:
"pet parents." This meant a fundamental shift in the
nature of the business, to becoming a source for services not just for products, sliding into a space where
Wal-Mart would not follow, offering grooming, vet-
erinary service, and eventually, pet boarding and
doggie day care.

Makes sense, right? But the managers in the
stores had been selected for and rewarded for their
distribution skills, for getting products onto shelves as
quickly and cheaply as possible. Now they were
going to be responsible for services—a radically different mind-set. That's why, at a time when services
represented less than 5 percent of revenues, services
became 50 percent of managers' bonuses.

I asked David Lenhardt (senior vice president of
services, strategic planning, and business development) about that decision, and he responded, "Services had been a step-child. Not only did managers
not care about them, they wondered 'Why do you
want us to care about them?'" So, when announcing

the heavy weighting in the bonus calculation, upper management made the case for why services were critical to the future of the company, then, as David put it, "We had the training and hiring pieces ready to go to support them. We didn't just give them a goal and a bonus, but the tools to help them get there."

The change in bonuses and mind-set meant a change in hiring, as well. One of the realizations that made its way into the hiring process was that the services business (which was, at the time, primarily dog grooming) had been attracting the wrong type of employees for the new business model. As David said, "The employees who applied to be groomers tended to be people who liked pets more than people." Now, instead of hiring experienced groomers, the company started hiring employees who wanted to work with people, then offered them a 14-week training course. Instead of interviewing for grooming experience, they began testing for verbal ability, asking questions like, "How would you sell me this pencil?"

(By the way, when I expressed surprise over the extent and expense of a 14-week training program for groomers, David explained that employees have to start working in the store, then apply to be a bather, then apply to be admitted to the groomer training. Once admitted, they spend 4 weeks at another store in training, then return to their "home store" for an additional 10 weeks of internship training.)

PetSmart's transition to a services culture has allowed them to resume their rapid growth. They are just starting to gain the synergy that comes from being the retailer for "pet parents." They now offer grooming and training, and you can get those while your dog is at doggie day care. Their pet hotels and vet services are likewise growing. Such a radical shift in the bonus structure led to a radical shift in the leader's mind-set. The bonus not only got managers' attention but also engaged their competitive energies. Upper management didn't just throw out a bonus, they threw out the ball and said, "Here's a new game—let's play!"

Number 32

You Get What You Pay For: What the Employees Believe They Get Paid for, Not What You Thought You Were Paying For

If you are convinced that you must start a pay-for-performance system, I should warn you that you will actually get what you pay for, which isn't always what you think it is.

Ruth Veloria of Charles Schwab says that the company's attempts to reward Customer Service reps have left "scars and bruises." In my mind, these are the sort of scars you can be proud of, ones to show off to others who are battling the twin dragons of bureaucracy and mediocrity—wisdom scars. For instance, the bonuses of employees of a call center were linked to customer satisfaction survey results. However, the employees were frustrated when they were assigned to enforce policies that confused customers—the customers took out their frustrations on the service ratings.

This meant adding another layer to the rewards system, providing an exception system where the unhappy client was not counted against the employee. However, even here, there was an unexpected benefit—a new feedback loop on how policies affected the customers. In fact, customer service is now part of the review process for what goes out to clients via marketing. So, what seemed like a weakness in the pay-for-performance system ended up being a strength.

A company started a recognition system where every employee could go online and report the good work of any other employee. The program was called High Five, and the employee being written about not only got the compliment but a five-dollar credit to be used at the company shop. It worked beautifully, except for the occasional abuser, like the husband and wife team that gave one another a ridiculous number of High Fives. What to do? This is where bureaucracy issues one of its alarms, urging management to write policies. However, the solution is not a list of rules, but for someone to pull aside the husband and wife and explain how the system is meant to be used and what it is meant to accomplish. You inspire them to use it wisely, not try to manage it via policies. Policies are a substitute for character, wisdom, teaching, and inspiration.

Number 33

When the Inspired Culture Takes over the Hiring and De-Hiring

When an organization becomes focused on circles of helping, the organizational energy begins to take over the hiring and de-hiring. For instance, the best reason to submit yourself to the rigors of interviewing with Southwest Airlines is because you have seen the energy flowing through its employees and you want to be a part of it. (One day I had just boarded a plane—*not* Southwest—when the captain announced we would have a 20-minute delay. One flight attendant decided to entertain the entire plane with her charm and her raucous laugh. She was so good at it that one passenger yelled merrily to her, "You ought to go work at Southwest.")

What is not obvious to passengers is how Southwest's culture also de-hires. I spoke with Donna Conover (executive vice president of customer operations), to verify that they have a six-month "fire-at-will" agreement, even with union employees. She said that they did. I asked how many people don't last the six months. She paused, then said, "I don't know. I don't think we've ever put together that number, but now you've got me curious. I'll find out." (Another example of the eagerness of gifted bosses to learn.) The next week she called to say, "I have it: 4.6 percent." She added, "But we don't capture why they left, so I can't tell you how many quit versus how many were asked to leave."

Donna went on to explain that her experience led her to believe that very few were shoved out by management, although some were shoved out by the culture. She gave me an example:

I used to work in reservations, and one day one of our new employees came to me and announced she was quitting. I was sorry to see her go and asked why she wanted to leave. She said, "You want me to be happy all the time."

I was unprepared for this, and it made me think. I told her, "I'm *not happy all the time. I try to be positive all the time, but I'm not happy all the time."* She *just shrugged and said, "Call it whatever you want, I just can't do it."*

•

Create an environment obsessed with positive energy and the culture becomes an incentive for those of the highest spirits to join the organization, while it is an incentive for seekers of the easiest possible job to walk away.

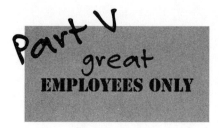

Part V
great
EMPLOYEES ONLY

Hiring is What You Do So You Don't Have to Manage (and It's What You Do with Some of the Time You Save by Not Having to Manage)

Number 34

Hiring Is More
Important than Sales

If you saw the movie *March of the Penguins*, then you'll never forget the effort each of those adorably awkward creatures devotes to nurturing a single egg. Well, that egg is hiring and the penguin is you. And like the penguin, the survival of your group depends on it.

I want to offer you a marvelous case study of how one manager/entrepreneur got his priorities straight.

Dan Bish owns the Norwalk furniture store franchise in Tucson, Arizona. The primary employees are the "designers," who work with customers and do the selling. Dan wants 8 to 10 designers on staff, but early in 2005, his store had a run of bad luck—one moved away, one took maternity leave, one burned-out, and so forth—and he was down to three designers. Dan bemoaned this problem to Steve Chandler, his consultant/coach. (Steve is the author of several marvelous books on selling and motivation. He has also been of help to me in my thinking and my work and has become a friend and ally.)

As Dan described his "staffing problem" woes, Steve startled him by saying, "You *don't* have a staffing problem."

When Dan reiterated his troubles, Steve said, "I understand that you've convinced yourself and your staff that you have a staffing problem, and that you have come to believe that it's hard to find good designers, but you don't have a staffing problem."

Dan countered by accusing Steve of not understanding the business: "Every store I know goes on about how bad it is—it's a huge problem."

Steve next asked, "If Donald Trump were to offer you $50 million to find 50 people who could match your top salesperson, and gave you six months, could you do it?"

Dan said, "Forget six months. For that money, I could do it in one."

Then, Steve completed his point: "So, you've admitted that the people are out there, you just haven't found them. So, you don't have a staffing problem, you have a recruiting problem."

The next day, Dan and his wife, Rebecca, sat with a legal pad and filled it with ideas. As Dan told me, "We sat down and came up with the list in April and, by summer, we had a waiting list of people to hire. By September, we were back to hitting our sales goals."

You're probably wondering what was on that legal pad, and I'll pass along the idea I liked best in the next section. (NOTE TO ANYONE THINKING OF

JUMPING AHEAD: Jumping ahead to the "solution" *is* the problem. The solution is not finding one good idea for hiring, but having the right idea about hiring, putting it in its place.) Here is Dan's revelation: "There is no magic bullet. It isn't what you do; it's that you *never stop*." For Dan and his store, this included: "Every Tuesday at one o'clock we have a meeting about recruiting. We discuss who is new to the list and who fell off. We get ourselves jazzed, every week."

Dan added, "Now, we treat recruiting as much like selling as we can. The company has all this data on sales—traffic counts and so on—and now we are collecting data on hiring." (Dan could tell me, for instance, that it takes 13 candidates to hire one designer. By the way, all the possible recruits are interviewed on the phone by Rebecca, first; then, if she finds them qualified, the candidates have personal interviews with the sales manager, then with Dan, and finally with one of the veteran designers.)

Once you have the data, you can no longer ignore the fact that the first step in hiring, as in sales, is getting people into the funnel, keeping the flow of candidates sufficiently healthy so that you can be very selective about hiring. As Dan puts it, "You can never think, 'okay, I have my staff, now I can relax.' You have to beat the drum, *all . . . the . . . time.*" Dan has reached the point where he isn't just trying to fill open positions but is "hiring for the bench," recruiting people to get onto his list so that he can have his choice if someone leaves, or if someone is "de-hired." (Reminds you of Lou Holtz and The List, doesn't it?)

The result is a gifted-boss mind-set that is indistinguishable from that of a great salesperson. (Indeed, gifted bosses sell the team — spotting prospects, getting to know them, learning how they could be of help, constantly working to improve the product and its marketing, generating word-of-mouth, getting referrals, continually following up, and making sure everyone is delighted.) This requires the sort of data the people in sales have. How many prospects do we need to spot and interview to make certain we have plenty of great employees ready to fill *any* open spots? How many prospects have we spotted this month? How many are we interviewing? Which sources had the highest yield of prospects and which source/type of prospect was most likely to yield great employees? Remember the wisdom of Edwards Deming: What gets measured, gets done.

Once you are treating hiring like selling, you can admit that hiring is marketing, and as sales is just one part of marketing, hiring deserves to be the priority.

Competitors can steal your ideas, steal your processes, even steal your employees, but they can't steal the magnetic environment that you, as a GEO boss, create through your talent pool, your standards and your inspiration. At least no one can steal it without finding a way to make you much better off by joining them, and in that case, I say to you, "Nice work. You deserve it."

Number 35

The Hiring Pipeline: The Best Selection Process in the World Is Only Capable of Picking the Best Person in the Competition

When HR departments, academics, and consultants do studies to evaluate hiring, they're seeking new ways to select the top candidates from the pool of applicants. A study will look, say, at all the employees still around after a year, go back and look at everything known about the candidates at the time of hiring, then tell you what factors correlate with employee survivorship. That's useful information, except it doesn't tell you anything about the people *you didn't hire*, and can't tell you a single thing about *all those great employees you never spotted or interviewed.* In other words, they can teach you how to pick from the pool, but can't tell you how good the pool is.

As a gifted boss, your goal is to get great employees into the hiring pipeline. It may take you years to hire some of those people, and some you may never get, but if you create the best pool of talent to hire from, over time you're going to learn the most about what it takes to appeal to the top people, and eventually, you will have the best talent. While hardworking managers are doing studies to see which job ads generate the most resumes, you'll be getting to know firsthand what motivates the sort of prospects who would never look at job ads.

You start with the open mind of the GEO boss—aperture, not closure—which means you are always hiring and that you never know where a great employee might come from. Again, it's just like sales—you might have more business than you can handle, but you'd be foolish not to meet with someone who could be an important client. You might find them so desirable that you make room for them, or maybe you learn they're in a position to wait for you. Open . . . always open.

●

Here's a terrific way to start to change your mindset, assuming you are, like most everyone, stuck in the old bureaucratic, hierarchical, parental mindset. It delights me to include an example from someone who works with one of the newspapers that has run my "Corporate Curmudgeon" column for over a decade, the *Albuquerque Journal*. Here, in her own charming writing style, is the wisdom of D'Val Westphal on developing a hiring pool:

I had watched other supervisors turn away applicants if they didn't have an opening at the time. You'd watch the applicant blanch as the proverbial door was slammed in his or her face, or you'd hear the short "we don't have any openings—click" phone conversation, and you knew the day would come, and all too soon, when an opening would arise, there'd be no qualified candidates, and the staff would have to suck it up once again for God knew how long.

So, when I moved into management I vowed to do a 180 from my previous bosses. I was honest with every applicant on the fact we didn't have an opening at that minute, but I always went on to say that didn't mean we wouldn't have one in 10 minutes, 10 days, 10 weeks, or 10 months. I emphasized that while we had low turnover and that's not what they wanted to hear as a job seeker, staff stability would mean a lot to them as an employee. And I told them I was always looking for qualified copy editors who really wanted to join our team, so if they were willing to come in and interview and test, we'd have the required preliminaries out of the way and could move quickly once that inevitable opening came up. If they weren't in town, I encouraged them to keep in touch, let me know where they landed, and I'd let them know about any future openings. I made it clear that I was willing to work on it if they were, and with both of us on the case, it would just be a matter of timing.

I hired at least five people this way—intelligent, talented, quirky, interesting people with years of newspaper or editing experience who targeted Albuquerque because of a spouse's job, family, or with an eye on the area's quality of life and plans to perhaps retire here. I took the time up front to screen them, and while I did spend time with people who weren't ready to edit the state's biggest newspaper, the applicants that ended up as hires were more than worth it. They were serious about wanting to work here—and in a stressful job like ours that's more than half the battle—and that was clear because they hung in there until we had a job for them. I couldn't have found them on a moment's notice, and if I had been brusque and dismissive during their job search, I wouldn't have blamed them for wanting to work for someone who valued their skills and appreciated their desire to work at our paper.

It seemed to me to be one of the few win-win situations you can set up as a middle manager—the current staff is happy because they know you're working to stay at full staff and thus you value them enough to not dump extra work on them if you can avoid it; the applicants are happy because you recognize their qualifications and are willing to take a little time to woo them; and upper management is happy because you're proactive and making an opening go away by hiring a qualified person. And in the world of middle management, the chance to make everyone else happy is one of the few times you get to be really happy, too.

●

What I like best about that story is how it demonstrates how easy it is to start a hiring pool — just stop sending away candidates. Does it take more time? NO. As D'Val lets us see, you merely *transfer* the time spent screening; instead of doing it frantically when an opening arises, you spread it over the year. Consider, too, that when you have an opening, that's when you as a manager need to pitch in and help the staff, making it the worst time for frantic hiring efforts.

●

Now, as promised in the previous section, let's take a look at the best idea from the legal pad of Dan Bish, our furniture store owner, and see how we can start to expand the hiring pool.

As Dan considered places and people who might help with hiring, it came to him that he had a wealth of colleagues who were business owners or leaders — bankers, attorneys, real estate agents, builders, and so on — people who understood something about Norwalk and about quality employees, and who could serve as talent scouts . . . *if* they could be enticed to do so. So, Dan came up with "referral captains," and a list of 50 people he aspired to have as talent scouts.

He didn't just call and say, "Know anybody?" Rather, he used his new insight — treat hiring like sales — and sold the colleagues on being referral captains. He sent a package with a coffee-table book of home interiors, along with a letter explaining that his store was looking for designers. He also stated that he realized that "To get good referrals, he and his employees had to be good refer-ers" and invited each person to send a stack of business cards so that they could pass them out to customers.

From that first mailing, Dan got five responses, and eventually made two solid hires. Some people might have been discouraged, getting just 5 of 50 people responding, but not Dan, who was thinking like a salesman. Next, he sent a follow-up letter, with a picture of the two people he'd hired, and a quote from one of the people who'd taken Dan up on the business card idea, reporting that he'd gotten so many referrals from Norwalk that he had more business than he could handle.

From that second mailing came another 10 responses, bringing the total of active referral captains to 15, and yielding a new star employee (a woman referred by the owner of a high-end men's store). What's most impressive is that Dan has 15 businesspeople as talent scouts, and he's not stopping there. He plans to do monthly mailings to all 50; after all, he's thinking like a salesperson and knows that he needs to remind people that he isn't just recruiting them to help him, but inviting them to join his circle of helping.

By the way, Dan also runs hiring ads, has recruiting posters in the store, sends out recruiting postcards to customers, offers a cash bonus to employees who refer a new hire, and even has a telephone on-hold pitch for new employees. But, as Dan is quick to point out, it's not the techniques that matter, it's the mind-set he calls "nonstop recruiting." His break-through was the realization that he must have a hir-ing pipeline and so, he has to create a "hiring funnel," just like a "sales funnel" where he can track the number of people that are going to be funneled into the pool. It gets measured; it gets done.

Number 36

Contrarian Hiring, Part I: The Underground Talent Market

One of the surprising findings in my study of gifted bosses came when researching those employees who were "best squared"; that is, the best employees of the best bosses. I soon found that most of these great employees come into the traditional job market only once, and some of them had never looked for a job.

What happens in the latter case is that their talents were spotted while still in school. (I found gifted bosses who teach college courses to have first shot at the best graduates, and others who have extensive intern programs or use a number of part-time employees.) More often, though, the great employees enter the job market, but only once. After that, their talents are spotted and courted. The two most common places that GEO bosses spot and court talent are from among suppliers and from random encounters with great employees. Other sources include the use of executive recruiters, or learning their skills and doing it themselves. (One simple do-it-yourself method is to call around to contacts in other industries and ask, "Who is the best _____ you've ever encountered?") Further, while a few great employees came from competitors, more came from other divisions of the same corporation, drawn in by the magnetic workplace of the gifted boss.

> If you establish a reputation as a great boss or as a place where exciting work is going on, you open the tap on referrals, where your peers say, "I met a woman at IBM who would be perfect for you." This becomes the "underground talent market"—a network of gifted bosses, spiriting away talent from ordinary jobs and into circles of helping.

The result of gifted bosses tapping into the underground talent market is that the stars almost never go into the traditional job market, rarely send out resumes or answer ads. So, if you are relying on a pile of resumes, you should remember that you are looking through leftovers—the folks that gifted bosses haven't already spotted and snatched.

Number 37

If You're Feeling Insulted Right about Now

Okay, okay. . . . Those of you who have spent a lot of time in the job market might be feeling slighted, defensive even. Good. That means there's an important lesson you need to go back and relearn. Your enemy is your Buddha, et cetera.

Sure, there are times when a tsunami sweeps through an industry and even the best are dislocated. Yes, there are plenty of solid employees who find themselves in the job market. However, I'm not talking about "solid"; I'm talking about effervescent employees—the people who lift everyone around them, the better-than-perfect employees. If you have been in the job market more than once, you need to examine if you are merely meeting your job requirements or if you have moved to the higher plane, joining circles of helping. If you have repeatedly entered the job market, it's a symptom that you haven't found your highest level of work, or that you have done a lousy job of making yourself available to the underground talent market. By studying how GEO leaders spot talent, you can make yourself visible to the best.

Number 38

Contrarian Hiring, Part II: Finding Unusual People in the Usual Places

What if you need to do hiring and don't have a sufficient supply from the talent underground? There are GEO leaders who find surprisingly good talent in the conventional job market, but that's because they approach it in unconventional ways.

Ask yourself, "What kind of exceptionally talented people might get stuck in the hiring pool, passed over by other employers?" For one, there are the people who don't interview well or who have something about their past or their personalities that is a "red flag" to conventional thinking.

Let us examine the case of Brooks Baltich, an insurance agent in Virginia, who tells us of the time he was opening his first office and wanted to hire exceptional support people. Another rookie agent had run employment ads, but had completed his initial hiring, so Brooks started by asking for the applications and resumes of the people his colleague had just passed up. It would seem that Brooks had no hope—the applicants were the people forced into the job market, and even these had already been picked over. However, Brooks says, "I tried to see past the resume into the hearts of the candidates, looking for what makes a true champion." It worked—Brooks' sales team has risen to the top of his regional group of agency teams. But how do you spot a true champion, I wondered. Brooks replied, "I simply look for different things than most other people do. For instance, one of the guys another agent had interviewed and rejected didn't dress right or look right—he had his collar up on one side and his tie was way too short." Brooks made a chopping gesture at his chest, adding, "just past his pectorals. But he had heart and determination and I listened to *how much he cared* about his customers. I hired him. And I'm glad I did. He is a champion."

Brooks' openness continues:

Another of my best employees came to me as a temp. A lot of people don't interview temps, but I do. And one of them was the worst interview I've ever had. She was so nervous she wouldn't look at me. She finally said, "I'm great on the phone." I said, "Well, do you want to go to your car and call me on the cell phone?" *She said she did. That relaxed her, and we were able to stay in my office and talk. I decided to take a chance.*

●

I spoke with Baltich's star employee, Dessa Eschmann, to hear the story from her point of view. When she told it, the plot was identical, but she filled in some details, saying:

I'm not nervous on the phone. I can call the owner of a billion dollar company and just do what I'm supposed to do, but when it's an interview—even when there's no pressure, if it's an interview for a job I don't really care about—I don't like being scrutinized, being stared at, having them look at every nuance of everything I do.

In fact, Dessa so hates interviews that she had chosen to work as a temp, because most of the companies didn't interview her. She only went to talk with Brooks Baltich because, "That week it was the only job choice I had."

We've all known bright people who freeze during testing, limping through classes or through certification exams, why shouldn't it be likewise with interviewing or the entire job application process? If you're using the typical hiring channels, you should pay particular attention to those who don't look or act the part. The opinion of the hiring manager, based on the job interview, is only weakly correlated with success. You could do just about as well in hiring without the interview. By consciously searching for talented people that *don't* interview well, you can find exceptional people in ordinary hiring situations.

Let's listen to what someone who is completely open-minded about employees sounds like.

Sheila O'Connell Cooper was an executive with both Mary Kay Cosmetics and Pampered Chef. She told me that when she was with the latter company it cost just $90 to acquire the starter kit needed to be a Pampered Chef Kitchen consultant. In other words, for less than a hundred bucks you're in a business where you can make a six-figure income: That's the wonderful raw democracy of direct sales organizations.

Because she's witnessed the success and failure of thousands of salespeople, I was curious if Sheila had been able to draw any conclusions about spotting great ones. She said:

The wonder of direct selling is that there is no type— not a personality type, not a way of communicating. Some are shy and some are masters of standing in front of people. They do share one common trait: a genuine interest in people, in helping others develop, and a willingness to step back and let the light shine on others.

(continued)

(Continued)

She added, "Most people know the difference between someone who really cares and someone just going through the motions."

What does a great employee look like? You know one when you see one at work. But this much we know: The best employees are not stereotypical. Being the best means that they have to be different. So, there is no reason to believe that they would look the part. Further, there is no reason to assume that they want a stereotypical employment situation.

Number 39

Contrarian Hiring, Part III: The Action Interview

Nearly all of us believe that we are above average in our sense of humor, our ability to drive and to judge people. It's the last of these that gets us into trouble with hiring. Early in my career, I was involved in a piece of research on credit worthiness; that is, on what predicted whether people would repay a loan. Among the *worst* predictors was the loan manager's assessment of credit worthiness. The best predictor? The applicant's phone status (specifically, if they'd had their phone turned off for nonpayment). The worst predictor was an opinion, while the best predictor was the hard fact of paying bills. That piece of research was a good introduction to my work in market research—testing products and advertisements—where we were routinely amazed at what went over and what didn't. The best researchers were the most humble—the ones willing to revel in surprise.

So, what does this suggest for interviews? Great-employees-only bosses understand that the interview is an artificial situation, where most managers ask the expected questions and get the expected answers. I recently spoke with a woman we'll call "Gina," a marvelous caring human being, who told me that she'd just fired her assistant (after two months on the job), and hired a new one. I asked what she had done differently the second time. Gina said proudly, "I learned my lesson—I told her *everything* I expected." And Gina went on to list all the things she'd told the applicant during the interview. She was proud of her candor; it never occurred to her that she had laid out for the job searcher exactly what she, Gina, wanted to hear. Sounds obvious, but we're all Gina's; we all hear what we want to hear and let interviewees know what it is we're listening for. What applicant with half a brain can't figure out what *not* to say and how to slide around the trickier topics? So, what you get from interviewing is screening out those with less than half a brain.

●

Here's the critical realization: *The person you interview is never the person you hire.*

The ideal is to go beyond philosophizing and see the work itself, which explains why so much of the hiring by GEO bosses is from suppliers or customers or via trusted colleagues and the underground talent market. However, some gifted bosses have found ways to see the work, even in interviews. One way is to make sure the conversation is about actual work— "Give me an example of when you _____ " or "Can you recall a time when _____ ?" Even better is to reproduce a work situation. One manager, when hiring salespeople, tests how they handle rejection by saying to applicants, near the end of the interview, "Well, thanks for coming in. I already offered the job to the person just before you, so I don't have an opening now, but it was good meeting you." He is, of course, looking for the person who takes that as a challenge, who wants to know what made the previous person so special, or who argues for hiring two people, or who wants to be the back-up choice, and so on.

There are aptitude tests for some jobs, and these are, no doubt, useful. But some wise managers are creating their own. Here are examples, told from the applicants' points of view (which allow us to get some sense of the delight in meeting a challenge that is characteristic of the best employees).

Raleigh Pinskey, who is now a consultant and author of the useful guide *101 Ways to Promote Yourself*, reflects on an interview at a time when she was "between careers," and a friend talked her into applying for a job at a hospital as a systems analyst, even though she had no experience in that field:

The Associate Hospital Administrator assigned to the interview process was puzzled by my application. After he described the duties, I assured him that one didn't need the usual Systems education to rewrite manuals or evaluate the drop in employee efficiency. Intrigued with my answer, he shared a problem: "Employees congregate at the water station, talking and wasting precious work time. What would you do to fix this situation?" [After looking at the facilities,] my answer was to provide the employees with bottled water, delivered to their desks with the daily mail delivery, ending the processional to the communal watering hole, which would be eliminated. I got the job.

I'm not certain if that hospital administrator really wanted to solve the water problem, or was looking to solve a hiring problem, but he hit on a tidy test—one that was easily understood by every applicant and that assessed not just creativity but applicants' attitudes about the nature of the workplace.

Let's look at what was certainly a test offered by managers who'd been wised up by a bad hire. This example comes to us from Debra Deininger, who now works with the American Red Cross Blood Services:

I interviewed at an organization for a marketing and communications manager position. Two persons conducted the interview, and there was nothing uncommon about the interview process, the questions, or the length of the meeting. If anything, I thought the interview could have been a little more extensive. I was not called back for a second interview and ultimately another person was hired.

About two months later, one of the interviewers called and said the employee had not worked out. Was I still available and interested in another interview? I arranged a meeting, expected that the two interviewers would conduct a more probing line of questioning this time around. I gathered more samples of my work, further researched the organization and rehearsed my answers to the tough questions I thought they might ask.

When I arrived for the meeting, the interviewer immediately escorted me to an office instead of the conference room where we had first interviewed. I started to sit down in the guest chair, when the interviewer told me to take a seat at the computer workstation. This was not to be another round of "Tell me about one of your workplace successes." The interview was going to be a real world test of my ability to produce materials under a time crunch.

I was given a topic and told to prepare a Power-Point presentation that discussed the myths associated with the subject and the realities that debunked them. I asked what reference sources I should use for the data. *"Your assignment is to find authoritative sources on the Internet," the interviewer said.*

The hiring manager answered a few more of Debra's questions, said, "You have 30 minutes," and then left her to work. The denouement:

The interviewer reappeared precisely when the 30 minutes had expired. She and another interviewer looked over the presentation and exchanged knowing smiles. I knew at that moment a job offer would be forthcoming.

There was a bit more of the traditional interviewing, but they offered the job and Debra took it and stayed until the organization lost its funding. She later learned that the person originally hired had "looked very impressive on paper" but couldn't come through with the work. Ah, yes, the person you hire is never the person you interview. However, the wise boss doesn't hire an employee but an ally, hiring the work, not the personality.

●

There are managers and/or HR departments who have come up with elaborative screening systems. Sometimes these are just more of the same, increasing the number of people asking the same useless questions. Some involve outside consultants, sometimes psychologists, and some use group interviews or aptitude testing. All of this is fine, but the real test is seeing the work, and this need not involve consultants or systems, just a bit of creativity (our next example) or a willingness to do a test work session (as we shall see in a minute).

One of the Cold Stone Creamery franchisees replaced employee interviews with a group "audition." Dave Siemienski, who has owned several Cold Stone franchises in Southern California (along with his partner, Howard Davidson), explained that he started auditions because he was so pressed for time that he didn't want to give up most of a day to interviewing. The audition process has evolved into a two-hour event, in which the applicants sing, show off, and/or create a skit about the product. It worked so well that it has become a part of the hiring process, companywide. I watched a training tape, showing the audition process, and the creativity was astounding. You could readily spot the leaders and the ones who took delight in entertaining others. (I found myself wishing I could go to a location and see some of these kids in action. Dave tells me that when an audition is planned, his current employees all beg to attend. Some do, and that way he is able to include current employees in the selection of new ones.)

The genius of the audition process is that it has leapt from asking about attitudes to bringing attitudes to life. Further, imagine the kids telling one another about the experience of the interview qua audition—the slackers will warn off the other slackers, while the most creative and energetic candidates will encourage their most creative and energetic peers to give it a try. And imagine the attitude toward getting a job offer after enduring such a test—it would generate pride and forge a bond with the company and coworkers, right? It takes on a bit of the logic of a fraternity initiation.

●

Speaking of which, let's look at the "initiation" for a thriving restaurant in Indianapolis, Indiana, called Hollywood Bar & Filmworks (they serve dinner and drinks along with showing movies), as described by Vicki Kenyon, director of operations:

The hiring process is long and drawn out, but it brings success. After an initial interview with me, the candidate sits with our existing management team (minus me) and they have a group interview. Each manager is asked to bring three questions for the candidate to answer. They also allow the candidate time to ask questions. If this goes well, the candidate is scheduled for a Friday or Saturday night shadow shift. These are our busy nights and it is a great gauge for me to see how they work "on the fly" and if they can handle the pace. Since we are a very small organization, this is all done in preparation for meeting the owner—she has the final say-so on all salaried managers.

I have put my foot in my mouth with too many bad choices to not do it this way. Our managers have a vested interest in the candidate's success if they assist in the selection process. It is a group decision, and that has value beyond belief.

There you see the attributes of a GEO leader: First, the company offers jobs that people really want; next, she has the humility to get other opinions and admit to past mistakes, leading by asking questions; and third, she sees the candidate in action. The result? If you go to their web site, www.filmworkson-line.com, you can see a list of awards, including a Service Excellence Award from a local business publication and a national award for being the "best marketed independent theater in the nation."

Number 40

Contrarian Hiring, Part IV: It's Not Just a Job—It's a Break

Another strategy of gifted bosses is to search for talent among those who are considered risky or troublesome. I do volunteer career counseling at the East Valley Men's Center, home to 80-plus men who have been homeless or in prison. I wish you could be with me as they talk about some of their employers— the ones who take a chance and give them not just a job but a break. One of the formerly homeless men I met at the shelter was a skilled carpenter who had worked for a terrific boss. He said:

I screwed up the best job I ever had. I started drinking, and I just took off with this woman and months went by. I lost everything and I was homeless. One day I was walking down Main Street in Mesa (Arizona) and this pickup truck slows down and then stops around the corner. It's my old boss. I thought he was going to tell me off, but instead he hugged me. We talked for a while and I explained why I hadn't called him—I was too embarrassed—and he just said, "When are you going to come back to work? Tomorrow?" And I did. And I'm never letting him down again.

Number 41

Contrarian Hiring, Part V: Hunting for New Talent Pools and/or Doing Pool Construction

Some GEO leaders discover great employees by finding new places to search for talent. Take, for instance, Bill Surrey, a contractor in St. Louis, Missouri. He wanted great employees but didn't have great budgets for salaries, so asked himself where he might find talent on sale. His greatest success has come via Family Services at Scott Air Force Base, just outside the city. He said of searching for employees at the base, "I found two types of people that I could hire—ones with pensions, who could make half of what they were making and be happy; and spouses, who would only be in town for two or three years and had trouble finding work."

Bill speaks glowingly of these employees, including this:

I had one woman who has an MA and worked in communications security. She retired because of a child, and she agreed to work 30 hours a week for me, with her picking her hours. She has created programs you'd never expect of a part-time employee.

As for the spouses, he says:

They go to most places to interview for jobs and hear, "Oh, your spouse is in the military? We'll call you." And they never hear back. They get bored. They'll work for minimum wage just to keep their skills up to date and to have something to do.

Bill says of his experience, "I've gotten great employees, with no cost for the help in finding them. It's the best deal in town for employers."

•

Other GEO leaders don't just discover new pools to dip into, but go out and build them. Here are two marvelously creative examples.

David Schlosser found a star by getting a referral from a surprising source. Here's how he tells the story:

I needed to find a corporate public affairs consultant in a particular state to represent the legislative and regulatory interests of a global telecommunications company. This was an election year, and the incum-

bent senator in that state was a prohibitive favorite, which meant that everyone who worked on his campaign would find gainful employment with the senator. So, I called the communications executive for the candidate I knew would win, explained what I was looking for, and asked if there was anyone he respected working for the competition who would be looking for work after losing in November. I figured that if a partisan campaign staffer could recommend an opposing partisan, I'd have someone worth talking to.

As it turned out, my brilliant idea for finding talent was almost a direct hit—the communication executive recommended a consultant working for his political party during campaign season, who turned out to be the best hire I ever made.

●

Next, we hear from Ed Leighton, the outplacement counselor we met earlier, describing his recruiting efforts for a Long Island outplacement assignment:

It was not even my job to recruit, but I knew we had a very specific niche to fill. We needed a mature, bilingual/Spanish professional with people skills, the ability to patiently train clients at all levels of competency, and who would be willing to be based out of Chicago and travel 80 percent. I found one . . . twice!

I sent an exploratory fax to every consulate of Spanish-speaking countries, as well as a few other professional organizations with ties to the Hispanic community. Within days, I got a call leading to a referral, then a hire. Good as he was, that candidate grew a little exasperated with the amount of document translation required up front. He left after a few short weeks. Fortunately, by then most of the translation work was finished. I sent out a second exploratory fax, resulting in a call from the wife of a consulate employee. Her husband was perfect in every way. He was smart, articulate, and willing to travel.

Sure, we might second-guess Ed's letting that first employee get away, but we have to applaud him for going out and building a talent pool. Here we encounter the "group brain"—you don't have to know where to find a star employee, just be bright enough to figure out who would know and then tap into that merged brainpower. You don't have to run an ad and hope, or go to HR (who will run an ad and hope); instead, you just ask yourself, "Who would be in a position to see terrific talent in action?"

Number 42

Being Worthy of the Best Talent: In the Long Run, You Get the Employees You Deserve

Julie Breninger is the veteran recruiter for high-tech companies. Should you, as an employer, fear her and the others like her? Absolutely. In fact, one company hired her in the same spirit that a high-tech company might hire hackers. This company had a chief scientist who was so essential to the company's future that the president grew paranoid about losing him. So, he hired Julie to call the scientist and try to recruit him, including saying that "the door is open," meaning that he could "name his terms, name his price." Everyone was surprised and relieved to find that this employee responded by saying, "Not interested. I love the work and the people and what we're accomplishing."

(Sounds like that was a chief scientist who worked for a gifted boss, although I would have thought that a gifted boss would have been more direct, just taken the chief scientist out for a beer and said, "I'm para-noid about losing you. What would it take for some headhunter to lure you away?")

Let me back up and point out that if you want to hire Julie Breninger to find you an employee, you have to pass her test. She lays out how she works, ex-plaining that she isn't just interested in the job to be filled, but in the *context* of that job; that is, the peo-ple surrounding the job and the dynamics of the or-ganization. You have to know not only what sort of employee you need but also what's important to you in the way a person works and interacts and convey to her "what's death to you." Then, she sets out her rules: When she calls, she expects a response within four to six hours. Once she locates an ideal candi-date, you can arrange an interview in a few days, and so on. She then says, "If you can agree, I'll work for you. If you can't agree, then I'm not the person for your search."

I'm no sales trainer, but I'm guessing that's a pow-erful sales close. After all, if you hear a list of rules, you figure she must be awfully picky about whom she works with, and everyone wants to be picked. But there's a larger lesson here—the best are picky be-cause they have the most options, the most "picks."

What does it take to be worthy of the best em-ployees? Let's look at how a "jewel thief" like Julie would go about stealing your best people. Julie calls prospects and ask this Zippo of a question: "What do you *not* have that you wish you did?" It's a question

you should ask your best employees before someone
on the phone does.

Julie says, "If you can't give them something
they don't have, then it's not a good recruit. If it's
just money, the next recruiter will do that again,
and they'll be gone." So, if it's not money, what
do great employees want? In her experience, the
common answers have to do with style—either
lifestyle or work style. In both cases, the issue is
often freedom:

*The companies that can offer flexible schedules, espe-
cially telecommuting, have a big advantage in hiring. Even if it's just working from home one day a
week, it's a big incentive. I have one man I placed
who goes to the office four days a week and then goes
to a cabin in the woods three days a week. He locks
himself in his office at the cabin, but still, that's a
major benefit for him.*

The other freedom is in the work itself—doing
worthwhile projects and following curiosity—and
in the nature of the work environment, as Julie
explains:

*If you want a star employee, you can't just say, "Get
me a star." Everyone says that. You have to let me believe that you have something special to offer. It could
be the project or the environment. One genius I
placed had a primary requirement for changing*

jobs—he insisted on working in a facility away from the company. He wanted to be left alone to work odd hours, come and go, and completely ignore personal hygiene. I mean, he stank! *He didn't shave, had creepily long fingernails and drove a car that was a moving trash heap, with stuffing coming out of the seats. Not only did they give him his own facility, the president went out and bought him some dress clothes and kept them in his office. He had a restroom in his office, with a shower, and he'd tell the genius he needed to come over and shower and change, they had a meeting with a client.*

●

Yes, if you want someone special, you have to offer something special. You have to be worthy of talent. In the long run, you get the people you deserve. So, as Shakespeare has a character in *King Lear* say in response to a compliment, "I shall study deserving." You start where the ordinary boss fears to go, inviting negatives and saying, "What *don't* you have?" Study deserving. The best employees expect to be paid well, and they deserve it, but they also need a good audience and a culture that inspires.

Number 43

If You Want Great Performances, You Have to Provide a Great Audience

In the ordinary organization, employees line up outside the manager's door, bringing their problems to the altar of absolution. As Steve Chandler puts it, "Most managers see their role as baby-sitters, problem-solvers, and firefighters. And so they produce babies, problems, and fires all around them."

In contrast, when I visit the offices of gifted bosses, I see the opposite—the gifted boss has employees who bring ideas and victories, not problems. The employees are showing off successes, not sloughing off responsibilities. The boss becomes a human scoreboard, lighting up as points are scored. The boss understands this correlation: the better the audience, the better the performance.

I don't want to pretend to have done psycho-analysis of star employees, but many of the best seek attention or approval. And I wasn't surprised when I heard James Lipton, the host of interview program *Inside the Actors Studio*, point out that one of the themes among his interviewee stars is that they come from broken homes:

●

"I'd like to thank my mother and father for providing me with the need to seek the love of strangers" (comedian Betsy Salkind, imagining her acceptance speech after winning an Academy Award).

●

Does that mean we must seek employees with sad stories of youth? No, but it's worth considering the psychology of star employees. The best employees are talented people who take joy in sharing their skill. As one of my best-ever employees used to love to say in response to a difficult task, "Impossible! It's a good thing you came to me." Stars want an audience. That's your job—to be a good audience and to direct the spotlight to star employees.

As a researcher, one of the most beautiful rejections I ever received was when I sought to interview a gifted boss, who kept putting me off. Finally, one of his aides told me, "It wouldn't be a good interview anyway. He would insist that he does nothing, that all the credit goes to his employees." His is the em-

bodiment of what we learn in the *Tao* (Stephen
Mitchell translation):

> The Master doesn't talk, he acts.
> When his work is done,
> The people say, "Amazing:
> we did it, all by ourselves."

Number 44

If You Don't Have A Great Story, You Don't Have Great Employees
or
a WOMPing Good Place to Work

If you want exceptional employees, the ones with glittering eyes, lively minds, kind hearts, and enormous talents, then you must never forget that they can get a job anytime, anywhere. Why work with you? Perhaps you represent the New York Yankees of your industry, with a storied history and budgets to match. Perhaps you are doing leading-edge technical work. Perhaps you are part of an industry with some inherent personal interest for employees. (For instance, if you are a devoted dog lover, you might be interested in PetSmart, especially when you learn that you can bring your dog to headquarters with you on Fridays.) However, if you are like most managers or entrepreneurs, you are limited in what you can pay, and you deal in ordinary industries with ordinary products. Are you doomed to work among ordinary people? No. You have a chance to change the nature of the work, to make the workplace itself something unique.

In doing so, you create what I like to call WOMP, which stands for "word of mouth potential." You want your work environment to be a story that employees will tell. As they do, they reinforce the notion that they work somewhere interesting or special, and they become a megaphone, sending out recruiting messages for you and your group.

When managers attempt to do this, they often take it on themselves to entertain employees—I think of the executive I read about who rode around the factory floor on a tricycle, handing out Popsicles. Not my personal style, but maybe it's yours. Then there are those who take the "servant leadership" notion literally and do things like host a barbecue and serve the meals to employees. Admirable, of course, but I want to suggest something deeper, a way of changing the relationship of employees to their work. I think of John Winzeler, owner of Winzeler Gear, who dreamed that his company would become "the Tiffany's of gear makers." He built an atrium art gallery as a lure to attract design meetings to their plant, and changed the company's image in the industry. He also created instant WOMP by having designers create gear jewelry and gear dresses, as well as gear-related artwork. You can see the implications for marketing, but there are bigger implications for employees and hiring.

Let me take a couple of minutes to give you an example of how I'd work if I were to meet with you and try to reinvent your workplace and make you famous in your company and industry. (This is part of what we do with The Innovators' Lab—meet with corporate teams in unusual places to come up with unusual ideas in marketing and management.)

Say that you manage the research and design (R&D) group of an industrial company making parts for heavy equipment. Fairly dull work, far from the glamour industries. So, we need to make the workplace creative if we are going to generate enough WOMP to lure great employees.

Because creativity is the process of forcing the brain out of its usual patterns, one of the "team brain-building" exercises I like to do is "change the game." We make a conscious decision to go away from the default model. In this case, the default model for workplaces is the traditional org-chart hierarchy that is the grade school model, which itself is derived from the military model. When I did creativity exercises for another R&D department, I started with a list of cultural phenomena that might suggest organizational templates—from Ringling Brothers to the mafia to evangelists, and I was able to use a few to make a fit to our R&D department. The one I found most immediately relevant is the Olympics model, however the entrepreneurial model has the leverage to change the nature of work. Other models, such as Disney, are less profound, and border on being merely cute, but they are more immediately applicable and might suggest starting points while fundamental change is being conceived. Here are the first three, summarized.

Olympics Model

An Olympics model would turn the department into a sporting event comparable to, say, a gymnastics meet. (Given that a lot of what happens in R&D could be called "mental gymnastics," it fits.)

- Projects would be awarded a "degree of difficulty" score.
- Each month, each team (or each individual) would come before the "judges" and give a timed update (say, two or five minutes) on their progress in the past month and be scored from 1 to 10. (The scores could be awarded by the leadership team or the entire group.)
- The "progress score" would be multiplied by the "degree of difficulty" to get a monthly score.
- A third score could be added — the feedback from the brand managers or other "customers."
- Monthly total scores would be posted, as would year-to-date scores.

  Everything would then be in place to:

- Keep a record book.
- Do a sports-oriented newsletter.

- Have medals or victory laps.
- Have team songs or cheers.
- Have cash prizes or other rewards.
- Recognize the "Player of the Week" and "Best Assist of the Week," and so on.

(The same effect of the "gymnastics" approach could be created by using a "rodeo" or "golf" analogy.)

Entrepreneurial Model

In an entrepreneurial model, a substantial portion of salaries would be replaced by fees. Each team/individual would bid on projects. The timing and pay for each project would be negotiated, with bonuses for early completion and penalties for going over budget or schedule.

This would create a strong link between productivity and income, without being judgmental about it. For instance, someone who had small children could work less, or someone could be semi-retired, and that would be fine—that person would simply choose to be in on fewer projects.

Disney Model

The Disney model would emphasize work as a way to earn vacations and to engage the family:

- Each team would be given a tough set of goals to meet by the end of the year. If the goals are met, the team gets two weeks off for Christmas and New Year (and it doesn't count against their usual vacation time).

- There would be a series of movie openings—films such as "Harry Potter"—where the company would arrange blocks of tickets and give them to the families of teams that were ahead of schedule and on budget.
- The movie tickets and other gifts would be sent to the employee's home, with a letter to the spouse or children, making the employee a hero.
- There would be special weekend events for kids while the employee/parents had special meetings or classes. There could also be edutainment trips—where the family is invited.

Okay, you get the point—to create WOMP while giving work some elements of a game. The model you choose influences the sort of employees you get—the first two would be pay-for-performance beauties, while Disney would make your department highly family oriented. Done right, the new model does hiring and de-hiring, while increasing productivity and morale. Compare this to the typical grade school model, which does nothing to ignite positive energy. Remember that the goal is to find self-managing people with terrific talent—the workplace should have elements that are worthy of such people. In the long run, you get the employees you deserve.

Part VI

~~EMPLOYEES ONLY~~ great

Understanding Bureaucrats, Upper Management, and Other Distractions

Number 45

The Unspoken Assumption of Bad Management and Bad Marketing

We are smarter than you.

Number 46

The Team Makes the Stars While the Stars Make the Team

We speak of "the Olympic team," but it *is* and is *not* a team: It's a collection of individual performers in matching blazers. Each performer roots for the others, hoping that the team will do well and the overall group aspires to coming home with the most medals. Then again, who remembers the medal count? No, we remember the performances.

An Olympic team is one way to think of those in any organization—a collection of individual performers. However, it is more likely that people on the business team have to work together—sales impacts customer service, which impacts legal, which impacts accounting. Most businesses are somewhere between the sort of team that goes to the Olympics and the sort of team that suits up for a baseball game.

177

You might be a star at your position, but you can't win without teammates. Win the World Series and all the players get a ring. On the other hand, if you win a World Series, you automatically create stars. But you don't get there without people who are or could be stars. So, we come to a bit of circularity that the best performers understand: The team makes the stars while the stars make the team. The most desirable employees don't just seek continually to raise their own performance, but also find ways to help those raise the performance of those around them.

It's tricky business to hire stars, not only are they rare—there's only one in a hundred who make the Top 1 percent, no matter how we pretend otherwise—but also because they are often prima donnas who use their talents for self-promotion rather than teamwork. After a bad experience with one such star, Dan Schweiker of China Mist Tea added a new phrase to the job requirement of new employees: "plays well with others."

Other organizations have become, consciously or not, antistar. They feel that hiring stars is simply not worth the trouble or risk. As one executive openly admitted, "We need middle-of-the-pack people." If so, then you have to settle into mediocrity or hope that your processes or patents are so exceptional and nonreplicable that they carry the team. But here's the catch: From where are future processes or patents going to come?

The goal of management is to hire humble geniuses—ones who want to be part of a team, which
means you're looking for 1 percent of those in the
top 1 percent. And you can't tell it from an interview—you have to see that unique genius in action.

This takes us back to Dan Schweiker of China
Mist Tea. This time we'll catch up with him by way
of his story of how he found in a high school work
program the woman who would become the company president.

Let me back up and explain that China Mist
provides tea and coffee to restaurants, including
P. F. Chang's and those in Starwood Hotels. Dan
and his partner, John Martinson, have been involved in community activities since they started
their company over two decades ago. One of their
early activities was using high school students to
deliver product. Many students came and went,
but one of them was special. Dan says that Rommie
Flammer didn't look like a great employee when
she started, being caught up in a "heavy metal
phase," but that he knew she was special when she
mentioned she saved every other paycheck she got
from China Mist. Further, she carried to work her
own standards. After working part-time a few
months, she dared to tell Dan that one of the ware-
house employees was slacking off. Dan, amused by
this, decided to try an experiment and said, "Well,
why don't you see if you can solve the problem."
Ten minutes later, she came back and said, "It's

taken care of. I fired him. And I hope you hire someone better next time."

Even though the founders of the company fit the profile of GEO leaders, the sort who rarely fire people, much less send a teenager to do it for them, they knew they'd stumbled across someone of unique potential.

Along the way, Rommie mentioned to John that she wasn't certain if she would go to college. John made the case for going, and persuaded her to try it. (Rommie, not John or Dan, told me that China Mist paid for most of her education.) She now has an MBA.

This is an example of how you can spot talent anywhere and anytime—how many executives would be chatting with part-time high school employees and learning about their financial habits, much less giving them challenges to see what would happen? But this example also shows the relationship of the team and the star. The team, especially John and Dan, kept giving their young talent new challenges, helped her evolve, and now she is helping those around her. The organization isn't as much hierarchical as it is circular—"circles of helping." The real stars of organizations are stars at helping.

If you're going to find humble geniuses, it seems to me more likely that you'll find them in a high school work program than in the graduating class of the Harvard Business School. Perhaps that's one reason that Wal-Mart has been so successful. One of the gifted bosses that I longed to interview was Sam Walton. Never happened, but, while I never got to meet Sam, I did get to spend some time with David Burghardt, who was a vice president in charge of opening thousands of stores, and who met with Sam at least twice a week for 20 years.

From my observations, the genius of Sam Walton was not his creativity, but his willingness to experiment. He was famous for visiting every retailer he came across and grabbing every good idea he saw. But he also encouraged his employees to experiment, telling his regional executives as they left meetings to go out to their territories, "Come back with at least one idea good enough to pay for your trip."

Also, adding more weight to my contention that the best executives lead via questions, not answers, David says this of his many trips with Walton:

I have this mental picture of Sam meeting with the associates in a store. He'd go in early, before the store opened, and gather the employees around and then get down on one knee and ask questions: "How's the manager treating you?" "What do we need to change?" And he'd pay attention, and he'd follow up. He wouldn't take notes, and you might not think it was on his mind, but then you'd get a memo about something one of the associates had said.

●

Further, David reports that Sam's two most common questions to his staff and other managers were, "What are you working on?"—meaning what *new* stuff are you working on—and the related query, "What have you tried?"

David added, "People would present ideas and Sam didn't mind testing any idea. He'd just remind people, 'Be willing to fail.' By that he meant that you could try anything, but if it wasn't working, admit it and move on."

I asked if the executives competed to impress Sam with their innovations. David chuckled and said:

There were a lot of outspoken people; they'd disagree in a minute. In a minute. And Sam loved that. But it wasn't competitive among the people presenting. We knew that the harder we all worked, the more everyone made. So, we all wanted the others to succeed. If you had a great idea, people would stop the meeting and applaud.

Can you picture it, a team stopping a meeting to applaud one of the members? That's a picture of a culture of succeeding together. How do you get there? Well, in Wal-Mart's case, everyone was getting rich. However, that certainly wasn't enough for a thousand other companies that started a great run and then collapsed due to internal struggles. Wal-Mart endures because Sam Walton was a humble genius. The born experimenters have to be, because they know they never know. That's the essence of "let's try it and see"; it's an admission that you can never be sure about an idea, and along with that goes the notion that a good idea could come from anywhere. If it can come from anywhere, then every employee everywhere is a potential source of genius. Every employee is a potential star.

Number 47

Your Work Is Only
Part of Your Job

You might think it a quibble, but I've found it quite useful to differentiate between my work and my job. For me, my work is my research, writing, and consulting. My job is something larger than my work, including all the accounting and contracts and forms and meetings. It's easy to start thinking of everything beyond my work as a nuisance and a distraction, so I constantly remind myself that the job is what enables me to do my work. Or, as I sometimes tell myself and others I work with, "You must do a lot of things you hate in order to do the work you love." This prevents me from self-pity, but it also puts the job in perspective. I mention all of this as a preface to reconsidering the relationship you have with upper management, HR, legal, and the other departments that seem to conspire to prevent you from getting to your work.

> One strategy for dealing with bureaucracy is the notion that it's "easier to ask forgiveness than to get permission." Sounds terrific; however, while glib, that statement always makes me think of the brave words of the general who ignored his subordinates warning him to duck down to avoid sniper fire, insisting "They can't possibly hit us from . . ." before falling over, fatally wounded.

Bureaucracy is a wily adversary, not to be under-estimated. It is part of the job, and an important part, in the sense that the beast must be appeased in order to allow you to do your work well. The best strategy is not to ignore the bureaucrats, but to entice them to join your circle of helping.

Take for instance, your desire to replace a second-rate performer with a star. You may find an ally in HR, like Pam Mix of the College of American Pathologists that we heard from in the discussions of pay-for-performance. More likely, you will find a gap between your department's self-interest and that of legal or HR. Odds are, those folks are content to have you keep a second-rate performer: Keeping any employee looks good in the retention statistics that HR might care about, and it means that there is no possibility of paying unemployment, or (the nightmare scenario for the bureaucracy) the expense and negative publicity of a wrongful termination or discrimination complaint. This natural reluctance of the bureaucracy to part with anyone is part of the genius of de-hiring—you help people move to something better, and even in our society of confused values, I haven't heard of lawsuits for helping people become happier. Your goal as a leader is to have the people who leave thank you, not sue you. You want graduates and lifelong allies, not enemies. Done properly, your de-hired graduates will ask you for advice and offer you as a reference.

Still, when people are coming and going, it's of interest to HR and possibly to legal. So, I urge you to ask their advice. Ask them about hiring star employees and about policies on firing. Know where it is they choose to get involved, so that you can either get their help (if they "get it") or know how to avoid their interference.

For instance, you might ask HR hypothetical questions about firing, getting to know their definitions of right and wrong. You aren't going to fire anyone, but there's always a chance that an employee will be so obstinate that you have to resort to firing.

I know of one case where a de-hire devolved into an instant firing. It happened when the employee said to the boss, "I know it's not working out and that you want me to leave, but I want to collect unemployment and I'm staying till you fire me." The boss—the owner of a small company who didn't need to wait for the

(continued)

(Continued)
bureaucracy to give its blessing—then said, "okay, you're fired." And they both smiled and shook hands and worked out the details. Even in this extreme case, the de-hiring didn't completely fail, because the employee was not surprised, angry, or embittered, and the firing was de-emotionalized and businesslike. I don't know that the two became allies, but they didn't become enemies either.

Just in case, you need to know about firing and lawsuits. All the world a stage? No longer. It's a courtroom, and anything you say can and will be used against you. That's why your HR department is going to want you to have documentation, and to make certain that you have not violated any written policies or done anything that could be considered discriminatory or unfair. In other words, they want to make certain that no one is fired until they know they have a legal case good enough *not* to get to court.

For those of you who want to get ahead of your HR department, or who don't have one, I have spent many hours with books full of legal advice, and there's one that I recommend to you above the others. It's from Nolo, the publisher of remarkably clear legal self-help materials, and is called *Dealing With Problem Employees—A Legal Guide,* by a pair of attorneys, Amy DelPo and Lisa Guerin. It has a nifty checklist for firing employees and a "when to consult an attorney" list. It also has easy to follow advice on medical and maternity leave and all the rest. (You can find much useful information at www.nolo.com. At the time of this writing, there's a "human resources" section that includes the checklist for firing.)

Most laws are meant to set a minimum standard of conduct—the line drawn by society that declares, "We expect at least this much." You, however, as a gifted boss, will have done more than anyone could ask to try to help a failing employee, have been more than fair, and you have come up with specific goals, usually with quantifiable targets. These need to be written so that they can be reviewed for progress and you have documentation. But, most of all, so that you and your employees have agreed to them.

When I did volunteer mediation for the attorney general's office in Arizona, I learned a useful fact that results from human nature. In our mediations, we would sit down with two people in a dispute, usually some matter that involved money but had become emotional, and we'd work out an agreement, which we would put into writing and have both parties sign. Some people worried that these agreements were written informally by people like me, nonlawyers, rather than written by experts. However, the statistics showed

(continued)

(Continued)

that people were more likely to keep these personal agreements than to fulfill resolutions handed down by the court. When people had an outcome forced on them—such as a court order—they might contest it, refuse to honor it, declare bankruptcy, or otherwise escalate the disagreement. However, if they came to an agreement and gave their word as to what they would do, they almost always did so. This is what the de-hiring process amounts to—coming up with an agreement on performance, you keeping your word to do all you can and the employee keeping a commitment to thrive or depart.

Number 48

Leading via Happiness

We first encountered Cold Stone Creamery in the early pages, meeting the man who inspired the "I ♥ Bruce" buttons that franchisees wore at a convention. We encountered the company again with their delightful hiring process via "auditions." Let me offer you some final bits of advice by telling you more about the company's leader, Doug Ducey, who embraces a premise of "profit by making people happy," and who says, grinning, of his company's culture, "We want it to be like our ice cream—smooth and creamy."

To create a "smooth and creamy" culture means flattening out the rough and lumpy in human nature, and that has led Doug to develop what he calls "adult conversations." He says, "We need to tell each other the truth if we're going to bring out the best in people." For instance, the company's director of public relations, Kevin Donnellan, says that after a public appearance, Doug will ask him, "How'd it go? What could have gone better?" And Kevin insists that Doug *wants* criticism, saying that Doug seems *disappointed* if Kevin can't come up with ways to improve.

When it comes to dealing with hundreds of franchisees, Doug has become skilled at keeping the conversation on what matters, ascribing it to "the dance of working with people." He says, "Any issue can be nitpicked. So, if a franchisee starts to second-guess a decision—the choice of a new flavor, for instance—I say, 'Let's talk about what's important: How are we treating customers? How are you doing financially?'"

The ability to keep conversations on key business issues is also what makes de-hiring successful. Doug calls his de-hiring process "counseling them out of the business." He starts with a single premise of assuming the best:

They are not bad people. With franchises, it may be that they romanticized ownership. "Profit by making people happy" includes franchisees. So, if they can't be happy, we counsel them out. We make it easy for them to transfer ownership, usually by having an existing owner buy them out. The transfer rate is about 10 percent. Our goal is that they can still look back and feel that they've enjoyed the experience.

So, the process fits nicely the ideal of de-hiring—doing what's best for the company by doing what's best for the individual. When I asked Doug about his failures, when the "counseling out" hadn't worked and the franchisees were angry and litigious, he was perplexed, trying to think of an example. He finally said, "I don't believe we've had anyone like that. It's not about personalities; it's about operations." Again, we see that when it's about quantifiable perform-ance, the process becomes drained of its accusations and resentments, and becomes what Doug would call an "adult conversation."

●

Looking back on what I've written about Doug Ducey, I can see that in reviewing his hiring and de-hiring, we have already established his philosophy for our third theme, inspiring. His example shows us how the three become one, that hiring, de-hiring, and inspiring are all part of a higher-order manner of dealing with people. In the case of Doug Ducey and Cold Stone Creamery, you start with a product peo-ple love and make it into an experience people want to be a part of. Done properly, the great customer ex-perience and the great employee experience merge into one. If you set a goal of "profit by making people happy," you have the underlying logic for hiring great people and de-hiring those who can't add to the chemistry.

By seeking to constantly learn — "How could it have gone better?" — and embracing "the dance of working with people," especially the "adult conversations," Doug has created an environment where people are reminded to focus on customers and performance.

I found myself being inspired when talking to Doug; you can see that making people happy makes him happy. Let's end with his metaphor of "the dance of working with people." Most executives think of business as a battle or a competition, but not Doug; it's a dance. Sure, some partners are better than others, sometimes you need practice, and there is a reason it's called "foot-*work*"; but, nevertheless, it's a *dance*. The goal is to enjoy it, for two people to enjoy making it work by making it graceful, getting to the point beyond pushing, to where it becomes effortless and everyone want to join in.

Final Thoughts

We all know that it is possible to succeed by being brutally efficient and coldly demanding. We also know that you can get rich by cleverly inducing greed or fear. What I hope you have come to see as you read the pages of this book is that you can create wealth by being warmly, kindly demanding, and that you arrive there by inspiring curiosity and helpfulness.

My work has thrown me together with hundreds of executives, and I believe that it isn't enough merely to put up good numbers; no, to qualify as a gifted boss, I say you must put up good numbers and good karma. A leader is admirable only by helping as many people as possible discover their most admirable character traits. Using money to make more money is a useful skill, but using people to make better people is the gift that the best executives share and receive. Those aren't employees; they are allies.

You aren't just working together; you are creating circles of helping.

●

So let's end where we started, with the chemistry of leadership success: 90-10-0. My wife Sandy pointed out that when stated as a naked formula, 90-10-0, it sounds like a fertilizer. Indeed. And that in turn suggests a useful, final analogy for a great leader—a gardener. The garden is your project, but the garden is also your professor. You start with great conditions for growing, add the best plants for the conditions, do some pruning and shaping, add water and nutrients, and hope for sun. You take joy in the results, but you never forget what the best gardeners know: Yes, it's *your* garden, but it's not *your* miracle.

Acknowledgments and Sources

This book was created from the examples and stories of the people quoted, and many others who, for one reason or another, are not directly quoted in the text. Some of those in the latter group who were especially helpful to my thinking included J. D. Farr, Brad Harper, Ron Heckenberg, Eric Shawger, Charles Berard, Terry Goldman, Matt Schenecker, Steve Green, Ian O'Connell, Charlie Oakes, Diane Greig, Robert Teolis, Dave Harrold, Matty Matoian, Jerry Knoll, L. A. Ellis, and Steve Lucido. There were others who asked to be anonymous, out of concern for the privacy or sensitivities of people who were important to their stories. I am grateful to all these gifted bosses and great employees for their time and willingness to join our circle of helping.

In addition to those quoted in the text and those interviewed off-the-record, I am thankful for the help of Janet Traylor, Bobette Gorden, Steve Brown, Steve Chandler, Bob Cialdini, Connie Denk, Paula Wigboldy, Joel Dauten, Sandy Dauten, my friends at King Features and at The Innovators' Lab, as well as Matt Holt and the rest of the good people at John Wiley & Sons.

About the Author

Dale Dauten has been researching leadership and innovation since his time as a graduate student at Arizona State University and then at Stanford University's Graduate School of Business. One of his early books prompted a government publication to call him a "guru" to White House staffers, and since then, his writings have been published in a dozen languages and have developed a worldwide following, especially in Japan.

As founder of The Innovators' Lab, Dale has done idea generation with dozens of firms, including Georgia-Pacific, United Auto Group, General Dynamics, Caterpillar, and NASA.

He also writes two newspaper columns, both nationally syndicated by King Features: "The Corporate Curmudgeon" and "Kate and Dale Talk Jobs" (with employment expert, Kate Wendleton). His work appears weekly in over a hundred newspapers.

Dale lives in Tempe, Arizona, with his wife and three children.

●

Other books by Dale Dauten:

The Max Strategy

The Gifted Boss

The Laughing Warriors

Better Than Perfect

●

If you are interested in bringing presentations or seminars on Great Employees Only to your team, please visit www.dauten.com.

Dale welcomes your comments and questions, as well as your experiences and wisdom: dale@dauten .com.